AF739212

The Global Evolution, Changing Landscape and Future of Financial Markets

The Global Evolution, Changing Landscape and Future of Financial Markets: From Traditional to Digital

BY

SYED ALI RAZA
Iqra University, Pakistan

DARAKHSHAN SYED
Bahria University, Pakistan

SYED RIZWAN
Iqra University, Pakistan

AND

MAIYRA AHMED
Iqra University, Pakistan

emerald PUBLISHING

United Kingdom – North America – Japan – India – Malaysia – China

Emerald Publishing Limited
Emerald Publishing, Floor 5, Northspring, 21-23 Wellington Street, Leeds LS1 4DL

First edition 2025

Copyright © 2025 Syed Ali Raza, Darakhshan Syed, Syed Rizwan and Maiyra Ahmed.
Published under exclusive licence by Emerald Publishing Limited.

Reprints and permissions service
Contact: www.copyright.com

No part of this book may be reproduced, stored in a retrieval system, transmitted in any form or by any means electronic, mechanical, photocopying, recording or otherwise without either the prior written permission of the publisher or a licence permitting restricted copying issued in the UK by The Copyright Licensing Agency and in the USA by The Copyright Clearance Center. Any opinions expressed in the chapters are those of the authors. Whilst Emerald makes every effort to ensure the quality and accuracy of its content, Emerald makes no representation implied or otherwise, as to the chapters' suitability and application and disclaims any warranties, express or implied, to their use.

British Library Cataloguing in Publication Data
A catalogue record for this book is available from the British Library

ISBN: 978-1-83549-331-1 (Print)
ISBN: 978-1-83549-330-4 (Online)
ISBN: 978-1-83549-332-8 (Epub)

Printed and bound by CPI Group (UK) Ltd, Croydon, CR0 4YY

INVESTOR IN PEOPLE

Contents

List of Abbreviations

ACH	Automated Clearing House
AD	Anno Domini
A.D.	After the birth of Christ
AI	Artificial Intelligence
AIG	American International Group
AML	Anti-Money Laundering
API	Application Programming Interface
APIs	Application Programming Interfaces
ASIC	Application-Specific Integrated Circuit
ATM	Automated Teller Machine
B2B	Business to Business
B2C	Business to Consumer
BC	Before Christ
B.C.	Before Christ
BCBS	Basel Committee on Banking Supervision
Big Data	Large and complex datasets that require advanced tools for analysis
BOP	Balance of Payments
CBDCs	Central Bank Digital Currencies
CD	Credit Scoring
CR	Cyber-Risk
CVA	Credit Valuation Adjustment
CX	Customer Experience
DeFi	Decentralised Finance
DFDM	Digital Finance and Digital Money
D-NY	Democratic-New York
DVA	Debit Valuation Adjustment
ECB	European Central Bank
ESG	Environment, Social and Governance

ETF	Exchange-Traded Fund
ETFs	Exchange Traded Funds
FinTech	Financial Technology
FIs	Financial Institutions
FR	Federal Reserve
FSB	Financial Stability Board
FTE	Full-Time Equivalent
FVA	Funding Valuation Adjustment
FY	Fiscal Year
GBP	British Pound
GDPR	General Data Protection Regulation
GW	Gigawatts
IBM	International Business Machines Corporation
IMF	International Monetary Fund
IoT	Internet of Things
IT	Information Technology
KPI	Key Performance Indicator
KVA	Capital Valuation Adjustment
KYC	Know Your Customer
M2M	Machine-to-Machine
ML	Machine Learning
MMFs	Money Market Mutual Funds
Mobikwik	A mobile wallet and online payment system
MVA	Margin Valuation Adjustment
NAV	Net Asset Value
Neobanks	Digital Financial Institutions
NFTs	Non-Fungible Tokens
NLP	Natural Language Processing
Paytm	Pay Through Mobile (an Indian digital payments company)
PKE	Public Key Encryption
PSD2	Payment Services Directive 2
QAOA	Quantum Approximate Optimization Algorithm
QC	Quantum Computing

QMC	Quantum Monte Carlo
Qubits	Quantum Bits
QUBO	Quadratic Unconstrained Binary Optimization
RBA	Reserve Bank of Australia
RegTech	Regulatory Technology
ROI	Return on Investment
RPA	Robotic Process Automation
RSA	Rivest Shamir Adleman (a public-key encryption algorithm)
SC	Senatus Consulto (with the approval of the Senate)
SaaS	Software as a Service
SEC	Securities and Exchange Commission
SMS	Short Message Service
SWIFT	Society for Worldwide Interbank Financial Telecommunication
SWOT	Strengths, Weaknesses, Opportunities, Threats
TAP	Technology Adoption Program
TRS-80	Tandy Radio Shack Model 80
TWh	Terawatt Hours
UBS	United Bank of Switzerland
US	United States
USD	United States Dollar
VQE	Variational Quantum Eigensolver
WAP	Wireless Application Protocol
WWII	World War II
XVA	Umbrella term for various Valuation Adjustments (CVA, DVA, KVA, MVA, FVA)

About the Authors

Syed Ali Raza is a Full-Time Professor of Finance at the Iqra University Karachi, Pakistan. He received his PhD degree in Finance from the Northern University of Malaysia. Currently, he is serving as a Director of Academics at the Iqra University North campus. Prof Dr Raza is also a Committee Member of the Ministry of Planning, Development and Reform to develop an Innovative Financing Mechanism under 'Ehsaas Programme' initiated by the Prime Minister of Pakistan. His wide experience of corporate and Academia has brought a blended knowledge in the area of Finance and Economics. He teaches at the graduate and postgraduate levels. His areas of interest include quantitative methods in research, energy economics, energy finance, financial economics and corporate finance. His research work has been published in world-renowned journals. The research work of Dr Raza has been cited more than 5,000 times in top tier journals. Prof Dr Raza is also a member of the editorial and reviewer board for many international research journals.

Darakhshan Syed received her Master of Engineering (MEng) degree in Computer Networks and Performance Evaluation from NED University of Engineering and Technology. She is currently pursuing her PhD degree with the Computer Science Department, Bahria University, Karachi. She is a Senior Lecturer in the Computer Science Department, Bahria University. She is an experienced Tutor of computer courses, such as programming languages, cybersecurity, artificial intelligence and software engineering. She was a Research Assistant with a demonstrated history of working in the education management industry.

Syed Rizwan received his Master's degree in Engineering (Computer Science and Technology) from the Harbin Institute of Technology, China. He is currently a Lecturer with the Faculty of Engineering, Science and Technology, Iqra University, Karachi, Pakistan. His goal as a Teacher is to ensure that students are well prepared to serve their society and community, especially as professional engineers or computer scientists. His research interests include machine learning, artificial intelligence, cloud computing and blockchain technology. He possesses good skills in MATLAB, Python and Weka.

Maiyra Ahmed is a Research Associate at the Iqra University Karachi, Pakistan. She received her Master's degree from Iqra University. Her areas of interest include quantitative research methods, financial economics and corporate finance.

Foreword

In the ever-evolving landscape of financial markets, we stand at the threshold of a profound transformation driven by unprecedented technological innovations. This book, *The Global Evolution, Changing Landscape, and Future of Financial Markets: From Traditional to Digital*, meticulously explores these dynamic changes, providing a comprehensive understanding of how the financial services industry is reshaping itself in response to technological advancements.

At the heart of this transformation lies the fusion of artificial intelligence (AI), blockchain technology and digital interfaces, which together are revolutionizing the very foundations of money and financial transactions. This book delves into these elements, offering a detailed analysis of their individual and collective impacts on the future of financial markets. It examines the introduction and integration of AI and blockchain with advanced human-to-machine interfaces, setting the stage for an insightful discussion on the future trends driven by digital innovation.

The current era of financial services is arguably the most intriguing in recent history. Rapid technological advancements are not only redefining the structure of financial institutions but also enabling new entrants to disrupt established norms. As with any revolution, there will be those who thrive and those who struggle to adapt. This book does not claim to predict the winners and losers of this turbulent time but aims to explore the driving forces behind this transformation and speculate on what the future might hold.

This work is intended for readers keen to understand the technological shifts shaping the financial services sector and the potential consequences for the industry and their own lives. It emphasizes the significant impact of four major areas of innovation: AI, blockchain (decentralized systems), the fintech revolution and the rise of crypto-assets. Each of these topics is explored in depth, providing readers with the context, history and fundamentals necessary to grasp these complex concepts.

In understanding these foundational ideas, readers will be better equipped to consider the future trends influencing financial innovation. The book posits that while AI, blockchain, fintech and crypto-assets each hold substantial transformative potential, it is their interplay that will yield the most profound changes to the financial system.

Beyond the technological advancements, this book highlights the critical role of inclusion and diversity in shaping the future of digital financial markets. New technologies offer vast opportunities for innovation and growth, but they also bring new challenges and risks. The authors present ways in which fostering inclusion and diversity can lead to more effective and responsible digital financial products and services, while also addressing the barriers faced by underrepresented groups in the digital finance industry.

Through detailed case studies, expert interviews and data analysis, this book provides a thorough understanding of the evolving financial landscape and underscores the importance of creating a more inclusive and diverse digital finance ecosystem. The multidisciplinary expertise of the authors – spanning finance, computer science and computer engineering – ensures a rich, diverse perspective on these critical issues.

The Global Evolution, Changing Landscape, and Future of Financial Markets: From Traditional to Digital calls on established scholars and emerging researchers to contribute to the literature on money markets and their transformation. It highlights technological innovations, shifts in customer preferences and provides insights into the future of money markets. This book is a valuable resource for social scientists, students, academicians, policymakers and other stakeholders interested in the future of financial markets.

As we navigate this era of rapid change, this book serves as a guide to understanding the forces at play and the future they are shaping. May it inspire further inquiry and innovation in the field of financial markets.

Syed Ali Raza
Darakshan Syed
Syed Rizwan
Maiyra Ahmed

Date: 25-07-2024

Acknowledgements

The creation of *The Global Evolution, Changing Landscape, and Future of Financial Markets: From Traditional to Digital* has been a collaborative endeavour, and we, the authors, are deeply grateful to everyone who has supported us throughout this journey.

First and foremost, we extend our heartfelt gratitude to our contributors. Your diverse expertise in finance, computer science and computer engineering has been invaluable in enriching the content of this book. Your interdisciplinary insights have helped us capture the multifaceted nature of the evolving financial landscape.

We are immensely grateful to the institutions and organizations that provided the resources and platforms necessary for our research and writing. Your unwavering support has been instrumental in bringing this project to fruition.

We would like to express our sincere thanks to our peer reviewers and advisors. Your critical feedback and thoughtful suggestions have significantly enhanced the quality and clarity of this book. Your expertise and attention to detail have been crucial in shaping the final manuscript.

Our families and friends deserve special recognition for their patience, encouragement and understanding. Your support has been a constant source of motivation, especially during the long hours of research and writing.

To our readers, we express our deepest appreciation. It is your curiosity and desire to understand the evolving landscape of financial markets that inspired this book. We hope that our work provides you with valuable insights and a deeper understanding of the transformative forces at play.

Finally, we would like to thank the publishing team for their dedication and professionalism in bringing this book to life. Your efforts in editing, designing and promoting this book have been exceptional.

This book is the result of a collective effort and shared vision, and we owe its success to all of you. Thank you for being part of this journey.

Chapter 1

The Essence of Money

Introduction

Money, known by various colloquial terms, is fundamentally significant. Despite different perspectives on its role, money's origin and evolution reveal its complex nature. Initially, barter was the primary form of trade, evolving into coinage and eventually into electronic money. Money's historical journey, from tangible items like shells and beads to modern digital forms, underlines its adaptability and essential functions: unit of account, medium of exchange, store of value and standard for deferred payments.

Historically, alternative systems like barter and slave trade preceded money. Barter had inherent inefficiencies, such as the difficulty of matching mutual needs. This led to the development of money, which facilitated easier and more efficient market transactions. Classic economic theories suggest that money replaced barter due to its convenience and ability to standardize value. While barter still exists in limited forms, the transition to a monetary economy marks significant economic progress. Notably, the move from barter to money was driven by practical needs for a more reliable and efficient trade system.

History of Barter

Barter is an ancient practice, predating recorded history, and is fundamental to human interaction. Barter, the direct exchange of goods and services for mutual benefit, is as old as humanity itself. Surprisingly, this form of trade still exists today, particularly in international transactions in regions like the East and the West. Barter is robust and adaptable, explaining its longevity and universality. When its benefits are carefully considered, its persistence in modern economies is less surprising. The primary advantage is the tangible nature of exchanges, as participants trade valuable goods and services directly without relying on paper money or promises.

Historically, barter was the sole method of trade, tracing back to the early development of money and finance. Our understanding of barter primarily comes from societies that existed without money in modern times. Traditional economic

The Global Evolution, Changing Landscape and Future of Financial Markets, 1–7
Copyright © 2025 Syed Ali Raza, Darakhshan Syed, Syed Rizwan and Maiyra Ahmed
Published under exclusive licence by Emerald Publishing Limited
doi:10.1108/978-1-83549-330-420251001

theories often exaggerated the disadvantages of barter to justify the evolution of money. Barter has been unfairly criticized and considered primitive in conventional economic thought.

As trade grew more complex, barter systems evolved to meet increasing demands until they were surpassed by money. One significant development in early barter systems was the preference for specific commodities as a medium of exchange due to their inherent value. Markets, often established before the advent of money, facilitated barter by providing centralized locations for exchange. Money eventually offered substantial benefits over barter, leading to its widespread adoption. Barter diminished but never completely disappeared, re-emerging during economic crises when money systems faltered.

Historically, barter and money have coexisted, with societies transitioning from barter to various forms of money over time. The study of barter requires an in-depth exploration of its components and its evolution alongside monetary systems.

Coin as Historical Data

Around 5,000 years ago, humans began using rare metals like gold and silver as mediums of exchange (Del Mar, 1902). This facilitated trade across different regions, allowing people to specialize in producing specific goods and trading them for these metals. However, the development of coinage was necessary to establish a more standardized and reliable form of money.

Origin of Coins

Oriental Cutlery

Around 1100 BC, the Chinese moved from using actual tools and weapons as money to using miniature bronze replicas, which were safer to carry (O'Bryan, 2013). Eventually, these replicas evolved into round coins, setting a precedent for coinage.

Coins and Currency

The first official coins were minted in Lydia (modern-day Western Turkey) around 600 BC during King Alyattes' reign (Toteva, 2005). These coins, made from a naturally occurring alloy called electrum, featured the ruler's image and facilitated more consistent and widespread trade, contributing to Lydia's wealth and trade dominance.

Early Developments (C. 650–490 BC)

Greek coinage began to flourish in the sixth century BC, with the Lydians pioneering the use of gold and silver coins (Mundell, 2002). Various Greek cities began minting their coins, often using symbols related to local culture and mythology, such as animals and deities.

Predominance of Athens

By the late fifth century BC, Athens achieved near-hegemonic dominance in the region, influencing other city-states to adopt Athenian coinage standards. Despite some resistance, Athens maintained financial supremacy, particularly through its silver tetradrachms, which became a widely accepted currency in international trade.

Greek coins are renowned for their artistic quality. Various cities produced coins with intricate designs depicting deities, mythical creatures and symbols of local significance. Notably, Syracuse and other Sicilian cities produced some of the most celebrated coin art, which was admired and imitated across the Greek world.

From Alexander the Great to the End of the Roman Republic (336–31 BC)

Alexander the Great standardized coinage across his empire, creating a unified currency system that continued under his successors, the Diadochi (MONIKA POHLE, R. A. S. E. R., 2007). This period saw the spread of Greek coinage styles and standards far beyond Greece, influencing regions as distant as India.

The Coin Portrait

Alexander introduced the practice of featuring idealized portraits on coins, a trend that continued under his successors. Initially, coins depicted gods and heroes, but over time, the likenesses of living rulers became common, symbolizing their divine or heroic status.

After conquering Greece, the Romans allowed Greek cities to continue minting their coins, reflecting a degree of local autonomy. Greek silver coins remained in circulation, and Roman adoption of Greek coinage practices facilitated the integration of Greek and Roman economies.

During Roman rule, most Greek coins were bronze, used for local trade. Silver coins were limited to important pre-conquest currencies for broader regional use. The major silver coinage, from Augustus to Diocletian, was issued in Alexandria, primarily for Egypt, and consisted of billon, an alloy of silver and base metals. These coins had Greek inscriptions and depicted the emperor on the obverse and various images, including Hellenistic, Roman and Egyptian themes, on the reverse. In Syria, silver tetradrachms were minted in cities like Antioch and Tyre though they gradually became less pure by the early third century. Bronze coins also featured the S C mark (Senatus Consulto) signifying production sanctioned by Rome. Significant local silver coin series included drachmas from Caesarea in Cappadocia, issued from Tiberius to Commodus, often depicting Mount Argaeus.

Several semi-autonomous regions continued producing their own valuable metal coins until they were fully absorbed into the Roman state. Notably, the Bosporus kings minted gold coins from Augustus to the early fourth century, which eventually degraded in quality. Similarly, the Mauretanian kings issued gold and silver coins until 40 AD.

Greek Bronze Imperial Coinage to AD 268

Under Roman control, various Greek entities minted bronze coins. In Asia, local Greek coinage continued until the governorship of Gallienus. While some regions lost their right to mint coins, others retained this privilege. Greek towns under Roman rule often featured local deities, heroes or symbols on their coins, reflecting domestic interests. Notable examples include Tyche, depicted as a goddess wearing a mural crown, and Roma, portrayed as a helmeted female figure. Despite the diversity in reverse designs, the obverse usually displayed the reigning emperor's head. However, exceptions existed, such as Alexander the Great on Macedonian coins and Hadrian on Athenian coins.

Significant coin series preserved images of famous statues, such as Phidias's Athena Parthenos on Athens' coins and the Apollo of Amyclae on Lacedaemon's coins. Local heroes like Homer, Anacreon and Herodotus were also commemorated. Coins often depicted important buildings and events, such as games and festivals. A unique example from Apameia in Phrygia depicted Noah's ark, reinforcing local traditions through coin imagery.

The Beginnings

Roman coinage evolved from Greek practices. Before the third century B.C., Rome had no coinage. Early Roman coins, attributed to Numa Pompilius and Servius Tullius, included silver and bronze marked with cattle symbols. Early Roman money involved coarse bronze lumps (aes rude), transitioning to standardized bronze fines in the fifth century B.C. Interaction with Greek cities in Italy introduced silver didrachms for larger transactions. Rome's first coins, issued around 325 B.C. in Naples, were bronze and marked for Campanian use.

By 289 B.C., Rome began proper minting, producing aes signatum (bronze bars) without value marks, displaying cattle. True coinage began around 269 B.C. with aes grave (bronze coins) and silver didrachms marked ROMANO or ROMA, leading to quadrigati coins during the Second Punic War. Rome's coinage evolved with silver coins like victories, featuring Jupiter and Victory, and smaller, devalued bronze coins.

Early Imperial Mint Policy

Augustus standardized Roman coinage, setting the aureus at 1/42 of a gold pound and the denarius at 1/84 of a silver pound, with token brass and copper coins for smaller denominations. Nero later debased these coins, a trend that continued with successive emperors. Diocletian and Constantine attempted to stabilize the currency with gold and silver coins, providing a foundation for future coinage.

Initially, Augustus' coins were minted mainly in eastern cities like Ephesus and Pergamum and briefly in Spain. The Rome mint resumed gold and silver production around 20 B.C., with Lugdunum (Lyon) becoming a significant western mint around 12 B.C. Official and local coinages coexisted, with the Rome mint overseeing broader currency needs, including frontier forces' requirements. Coins continued to display the emperor's image and symbols of Roman authority and military glory. As Christianity spread, symbols like the chi-rho monogram began appearing on coins, culminating in Christian motifs under Constantine.

Coinage in Western Continental Europe, Africa, and the Byzantine Empire

The Byzantine Empire maintained gold currency dominance in Europe for a millennium, competing with Arab caliphates and Italian republics. Germanic rulers in Western Europe adopted Roman monetary systems, with gold coins reflecting Byzantine influences. Local variations in coin design emerged, with regions like Spain producing elegant coins, while those from Africa and Britain were considered artistically inferior. The weight and purity of gold coins remained relatively stable despite economic turmoil.

Later Mediaeval and Modern Coinages of Continental Europe

The 10th-century transition from Frankish to German rulers saw the spread of the silver denier across Europe. Byzantine decline led to gold coinage debasement, but Italian cities revived gold coinage in the 13th–14th centuries. This led to the need for higher-denomination silver coins like the grosso. By the 15th century, mechanical coining techniques emerged, becoming widespread by the 16th century. The influx of New World gold and silver necessitated token coinages in the 17th century. By the 19th century, Europe adopted gold standards, with paper money redeemable in gold becoming common.

Techniques of Production

Metal's durability and malleability made it ideal for currency. Casting, initially the primary method, was complemented by striking to prevent counterfeiting. Greek coinage began with electrum pellets stamped with a punch. Roman coinage evolved from cast bronze bars to struck bronze, silver and gold coins, with debasement starting under Nero. The need to finance state expenses led to the widespread debasement of coinage, contributing to Rome's economic decline.

Paper Money

To address the risks of holding large amounts of metal, paper money emerged in China over 1,000 years ago and spread globally by the 18th and 19th centuries

(Del Mar, 1902). Initially backed by gold or silver, banknotes and deposits became claims to metal reserves. Banks could lend more than their metal holdings, leading to economic instability when borrowers defaulted.

Summary

The significance of money, humourously overstated as making the world go round, has deep historical roots and a complex evolution. From barter systems to electronic forms, money's role has always been more than economic, encompassing emotional and social dimensions. Barter, an ancient practice still in limited use, highlighted inefficiencies that led to the development of money, facilitating easier and more efficient trade. Early forms of money, like shells and beads, evolved into coins made of precious metals, marking significant progress.

Coins, first used around 5,000 years ago, became standardized mediums of exchange. Lydia, in modern-day Turkey, is credited with minting the first official coins around 600 BC. These coins, made of electrum, featured the ruler's image and promoted trade. Greek coinage, beginning around 650–490 BC, saw various cities minting their coins, often depicting local culture and mythology. Athens achieved dominance with its silver tetradrachms, influencing other city-states and facilitating widespread trade.

Greek coins were known for their artistic quality, depicting deities, mythical creatures and local symbols. Alexander the Great's conquests further standardized coinage, spreading Greek styles and standards far and wide. The Romans continued this tradition, allowing Greek cities to mint coins under their rule, integrating Greek and Roman economies.

Under Roman rule, Greek coinage continued, primarily in bronze for local trade and limited silver coinage for regional use. The chapter discusses the evolution of Roman coinage policies and the spread of coinage across Western Europe, Africa, and the Byzantine Empire. The Byzantine Empire maintained gold currency dominance for a millennium, while Italian cities revived gold coinage in the mediaeval period.

Paper money emerged over 1,000 years ago in China, spreading globally by the 18th and 19th centuries. Initially backed by metal reserves, paper money allowed for more flexible economic systems. Banks could lend more than their metal holdings, leading to economic instability when borrowers defaulted.

Money's role extends beyond economic transactions, influencing social behaviours, attitudes and opportunities. While some view money with contempt or excessive concern, it remains a fundamental component of modern life. The transition from barter to money allowed for economic development and the rise of market economies, significantly impacting underdeveloped regions.

The rise of coinage marked a shift from barter and other primary forms of money. Coins provided a standardized and reliable form of currency, facilitating trade and economic growth. The history of coins, particularly in ancient Greece and Rome, highlights their role in shaping economies and cultures.

In conclusion, money's significance has evolved from ancient barter systems to modern electronic forms. Its role in society extends beyond economics, encompassing emotional and social dimensions. The development of coins and paper money marked significant milestones in human history, reflecting the changing needs and complexities of trade and commerce.

Learning Objectives

(1) To understand the concept and origin of bartering.
(2) To understand the nature and functions of money.
(3) To recognize the importance of coins as a source of evidence of past events and the historical context they convey.
(4) To explore the shift in value and trade from a variety of trade goods to standardized coinage.
(5) To demonstrate the change in currency from Greek hegemony to Roman influence.
(6) To elaborate the processes used in coin development over time.

Chapter 2

The Growth of Business and Economic Matters

Introduction

Progressively, governments acted as managing and regulating bodies. The government had the authority to specify legal tender, outlining the kind of payment which lawfully settled/satisfied a liability when proposed to the creditor, which might be utilized to payoff taxes. Additionally, government fixed the weight and metal arrangement of coins. Afterwards, these coins were substituted with a bill of exchange (assurances to reimburse in gold or silver) which was later termed as 'fiat money' (dollar bill) that were produced on the authorization of the independent power or authority in government, later quantified to be various dollars, pounds or yen and others.

Initially, the important production of paper money took place in France in the 18th century. Later, the assignats were issued by the French Revolutionary governments during 1789–1796.

Likewise, the American colonies and afterwards the Continental Congress introduced credit bills which could be utilized to settle debts and for payments.

These early inventions and experiments were termed fiat money which was excessively issued leading to increasing the prices drastically till the money turned useless. Either these were exchanged in token money (metallic money) at a minor portion of its original value.

Consequently, production and supply of fiat money in the main economies in 19th century were provisional withdrawals from a metallic criterion. For instance, in Great Britain, the government deferred gold payments for all unsettled dollar bills from 1797 to 1815 – Napoleonic Wars (Duckenfield, 2016). For war financing, the government dispensed fiat paper bills. As a result, the prices multiplied; ultimately, gold and silver coins increased enormously with reference to paper money in Great Britain. In order to reestablish the gold specification at the previous gold prices, the government reduced the price standard through decreasing the level of money. In Great Britain (1821), the specifications of gold were re-established. Likewise, at the time of American Civil Wars, the government of the United States postponed the conversion of paper money into gold or

The Global Evolution, Changing Landscape and Future of Financial Markets, 9–16
Copyright © 2025 Syed Ali Raza, Darakhshan Syed, Syed Rizwan and Maiyra Ahmed
Published under exclusive licence by Emerald Publishing Limited
doi:10.1108/978-1-83549-330-420251002

silver coins, and recontinuation did not take place till 1879 (McCandless, 1996). In 1864, the paper money price in terms of gold, technically equalled to 100 dollars, inflated higher than 250 dollars.

Such sort of events began to reoccur frequently in various region which persuaded people that war leads inflation and after effects result as deflation and depress. The following order was not unavoidable. It mirrored the experience of 19th century having metallic monetary criteria. Usually, wars need higher government spending and budget shortfalls. Governments put off the gold/metallic criteria and backed their shortfalls through loans and issuing paper money. Subsequently, prices skyrocketed.

During the course of history, the gold prices became far beyond their postwar value when time of war spending and inflation came to an end. In order to retain the metallic worth to the gold's postwar worth in paper money, price estimated in paper money had to decrease. The substitute was to approve the surge in gold prices against paper money through undervaluing the currency (which denoted to decreasing purchasing power of money). When the World War I (WWI) ended, the British and the US governments stressed prices to decrease; however, various other economies undervalued their currencies in terms of gold. Later World War II (WWII), all chief economies approved the increased price level of wartime, and majority of them undervalued their bills to evade deflation.

The extensive utilization of paper money created other issues. Like the expense of generating paper money was immensely less than its exchange worth, counterfeiting was usual as it used to cost around 4 cents to make a single US paper currency piece in 1999. Afterwards, the advancement of replicating machines required modifications in paper and the utilization of metallic bands and other instruments to produce counterfeit more tough. Additionally, the machines use to recognize, tally or modify currency amplified the demand for assessments to recognize original currency.

Standards of Value

During the mid-ages, when money contained coins mainly, silver and gold coins disseminated concurrently. As government took over the coinage and particularly as fiat money presented, the face value of fait money was specified in monetary units against silver/gold fixed weights. While some accepted a national bimetallic standard that fixed the weights of gold and silver based on their relative values, such as establishing that 15 ounces of silver would be equivalent to 1 ounce of gold. When the prices fluctuated, the situation connected with 'Gresham's law' which guaranteed the bimetallic measures sank into monometallic measures. For instance, silver's quantity nominated as the equal to monetary unit of 1 ounce of gold, i.e. 15 to 1 which was fewer than the quantity that might be acquired in the market for 1 ounce of gold let say 16 to 1 (Elwell, 2011). Therefore, no one would agree to turn the gold into coins. Acquirers of gold for the sake of profit would purchase silver in the market, obtaining 16 ounces for every ounce of gold as they would be the holder of 15 ounces of silver to the mint to be coined and used for gold payment.

Persisting this method for profit making, the following exchange excluded gold from mint, leaving behind silver in the mint for coining. Due these on-going scenarios, silver as the inexpensive metal forced out gold and became the standard. This event occurred in various regions of Europe, and so till the 19th century, all economies accepted the silver standard. However, in Britain, the ratio followed was set in the 18th century by the orders of Sir Isaac Newton (at time positioned as mint master) that overrated gold and hence directed to an efficient gold calibre. While on the other hand, in the United States, the ratio of 15 silver ounces to 1 gold ounce was fixed in 1792. It overrated silver; therefore, the new standard was silver. But the ratio was changed to 16 to 1 in 1834 that hyped gold and so again gold became the calibre.[1]

The Decline of Gold

But various issues were connected with this phenomenon like decline in the price of gold.

The real international gold criteria successfully concluded after WWI. Majority of the hostile countries deferred the unrestricted exchange of gold. The United States, later it entered into the war, continued exchange and thus banned the export of gold. After some years when the war ended, several economies had non-exchangeable national bill calibre, which means the un-exchangeable paper money could not to transformed or changed into gold/silver. The exchange rate among currencies set as the market rate deviated continuously. It was considered an interim occurrence, such as the deferral of gold payments by British government at the time of Napoleonic period. Although the prime purpose was to reestablish the postwar gold standard, economic instability and fluctuating exchange rates made it difficult to achieve a consistent and reliable monetary system. Meanwhile, an increase in monetary value was reported in various economies at the time of the war, further economies had to accept devaluation and depression in order to reestablish gold standard. Such act controlled monetary enhancements for the period 1920.

Moreover, Britain being persistent as financially strong favoured devaluation. In 1925, Winston Churchill (chancellor of Exchequer) chose to accept dominant financial arrangement and follow the postwar parity such as pound sterling was again set as equivalent to 123.274 grains of gold 11/12 fine (Duignan, 2012). It influenced exchange rates (current prices in Britain) leading to overrating the pound, resulting to generate gold outflows, particularly, later France selected reduction/deflation and restored gold standards in 1928 at a parity which devalued Franc. During 1929, the chief currencies of the globe and strong to weak ones all began to again back to gold.

---

[1]https://www.decaturjewelry.com/2023/02/09/the-gold-to-silver-ratio-what-does-it-mean/

The gold standards which were reestablished, although, were different from the postwar gold standards. The construct of the Federal Reserve System in the United States was established in 1914 that was a supplementary support to the international specie-flow process. This process cannot further operate mechanically as it can function only if the Federal Reserve (FR) approves this process and stress upon it. But if the FR didn't approve, in order to avoid local prices from increasing, it equalizes the impact on the level of money leading rise in the gold also known as sterilized monetary impact.

France selected akin alternative, resulting in the devaluation of franc directing gold being poured to the economy. The government of France vended the forex market for the sake of gold, flowing out the gold from Britain and different gold standard economies. The economies getting gold were the United States and France, which restricted the inflow of gold to regulate their prices. Economies which drained gold had to suffer from deflation. Hence, the exchange level of gold pushed deflation and deprivation by various economies. In 1929, recession made its way to Britain and Germany which further penetrated to the United States making the condition worse. Later, the recession was termed as 'the Great Depression'.

Moreover, in 1931, Japan and Britain dismissed the standards of gold, following the Scandinavian economies and various other territories in the British rule, such as Canada. Later, in 1933, the United States reestablished a fixed, however a higher value of dollar for gold, i.e. 35 USD against 1 ounce, discouraging people to purchase or hold gold (Peden, 1983). Finally, in 1936 Belgium, France, Italy and Switzerland also dismissed gold standards. Thus, in those times, it was not obvious that the gold standards were near to termination.

The Bretton Woods System

At the time of WWII, Britain and the United States defined the monetary system after the war. The economies' plan was accepted by more than 40 economies at the 'Bretton Woods Conference' held in 1944 July (Rofe, 2017). The conference's purpose was to highlight the alleged shortage of the postwar gold exchange level comprising of the floating exchange rate volatility, the fixed exchange standard inflexibility and dependence on an altered system for economies having surplus payments/deficits. Hence, these issues were frequently solved through recession/deflation in deficit economies combined with development and inflation in surplus economies. Further, the contract output from the conference directed the formation of 'IMF – International Monetary Fund'; the economies became part through paying subscription. The subscribed economies accepted to regulate a fixed system with adaptable exchange rates. Economies facing deficit in payments can borrow funds whereas the ones with excess resources can finance. But if the deficit/surplus continued, the contact offers exchange rate changes. In 1947, the IMF started to function with the USD being the reserve currency for funds and the gold price was fixed at 35 USD for one ounce. The United States approved to regulate the price through gold buying and selling (Triffin, 1978).

Recovery after the war, less inflation, the expansion of trade and maintaining international reverses in industrial economies offered the novel structure to function completely in 1958. However, a residual connection to gold persisted with the gold rate fixed at 35 USD to 1 ounce; the Bretton Woods system considerably levelled the economies' market on a dollar standard. In short, the USD became the principal currency worldwide and economies maintained their reserves and investments in USD.

The USD was extensively used in various domains like international trade, and the other currencies were measured against USD. Economies regulated their authorized exchange standard via USD purchasing and selling. The presence of the USD did not stop other economies from diversifying their exchange rates, similar to the gold which did not limit the currency to depreciate or inflate against gold. But for the United States to maintain the fixed price of gold became highly challenging, various economies depreciated or increased their currencies, such as strong economies named UK, Germany and France. On the other hand, the United States was not eligible to set their own exchange rate/BOP standards. In the United States, the monetary growth offered reserves for other economies, facing monetary issues. In early years, the central banks were authorized to convert USD into gold, which they did. Thus, the USD reserve within Central bank increased while the gold reserve in the United States decreased due to which the United States could not fulfil its agreement to change gold into USD at the agreed rate of 35 USD. Therefore, the system named Bretton Woods (fixed exchange rate) failed. However, government and central banks tried to prolong itss life but due to conflict of interest, no solution could be found. The Bretton Woods system was finally terminated in 1971, after the President Richard M. Nixon stated that the United States would not sell gold.[2]

After Bretton Woods

The end of fixed exchange rate standard terminated the economies' restriction to regulate the fixed rate of its currency in term of gold or others. Through Bretton woods, the currency of a country floated, which means that the exchange rate operates on demand of the market that can appreciate or depreciate the currency's value. While if the currency appreciates, buyers earn less amount of local money in return for an amount of their local currency. The buyers of local goods, services or assets bear higher rates. On the contrary, if currency depreciates, local services and commodity price reduces for people living abroad. Economies which were highly reliant on external trade disapproved the rapid deviation in price and costs in the latest floating prices. At times, government authorities and central banks usually interfered to relax deviation in the nominal exchange rate. Classically, such actions had been useful but only against brief deviations.

In long term, an economy's exchange mechanism operates in the basic elements like productivities' growth, investment opportunities, public saving and policies related to monetary and fiscal system. Such basic elements are fundamental to an economy either it implements fixed or floating exchange system. Further, the authorities interfere to regulate or relax the exchange rate fluctuations. Considering,

---

[2]https://www.investopedia.com/terms/b/brettonwoodsagreement.asp

the markets for commodities, services and investment, forex market should be analyzed as the economies must regulate the market.

Moreover, the prime difference of fixed and floating exchange system is based on the economy's regulation and administration. The fixed exchange mechanism changes take place usually when cost/prices of numerous commodities and products fluctuate, produced domestically. Whereas floating exchange rate changes take place due to deviation in the nominal exchange rates. For instance, the monetary policy of Brazil escalates inflation, locally manufactured shoes, cocoa and everything will increase. While, with the fixed exchange rate, the cost increase discourages exports and overseas purchase, the demand will shift from Brazil to different economies and reduce demand and earnings from locally manufactured products leading to reduction in the money stock of Brazil. The decrease in money and demand pushes the economy towards depression, leading to reduce prices. Whereas, in case of floating exchange rate, the reconciliation occurs through decreasing the demand of currency and exchange rate depreciation, hence decreasing the price foreigners pay.

Reconciliation can be done in various other manners. In the stated scenario, Brazil can opt for investment in overseas market, or financers might invest a less in the economy. The future results will be similar as the buyers and sellers would not consider the nominal exchange rare. The considerable issue is the alleged real exchange rate/nominal exchange rate reconciled through prices locally and overseas. Such as the Brazilian shoes buyer in England would only consider the shoe cost in British Pound – GBP. The Brazilian shoes price is increase through the exchange rate to meet the price of the United Kingdom. With floating exchange rates, the rates are reconciled to maintain an economy's product and services prices comparative to the market, globally.

Later in 1973, when the Bretton Woods system concluded, various economies opted for floating exchange rates for currencies; however, this setting was changed again. Typically, smaller economies based majorly on trading industry disapproved float system. Such economies demanded to reduce the regular fleeting but higher deviation in costs and prices increasing in the forex market. Majority of the smaller economies within Asia, Central America and Caribbean fixed their exchange rates against USD. Others like Netherlands and Austria fixed their exchange rates equivalent to German Mark due to extensive trading with Germany. As these economies stopped implementing central bank independent policies, hence when the US Federal Reserve or Bundesbank fluctuate interest rates, economies with fixed exchange rates in German Mark or the USD also changed their interest rates.

An economy with a fixed exchange rates surrendered an independent monetary plan. But sometimes, the surrender was compulsory; thus, a small economy highly dependent on trading with foreign countries has limited scope for an independent monetary policy. This could not affect prices mostly particularly the buying and selling ones. However, if the central banks or government increases their prices, the currency value decreases to boost its local cost back equalize with global market levels. Also, the developed economies could not regulate independent monetary policies with fixed exchange rates and capital market being open to inflow and outflow of funds. In 1980, due to the less dependence on capital controls, various economies ended fixed exchange rate to have at least some control on domestic monetary policy. But these changes were reversed back by the end of the 20th century.

Developed economies like the United States, the United Kingdom and Japan were still operating on the float exchange rate and so did the Canada and Switzerland (Bordo, 2003). Although these two economies were developing, they chose to have some control over their domestic policies. On the other hand, Hong Kong preferred a diverse selection of fixed exchange rate against USD. The system modification took place in 19th century known as a currency board. In this system, there was no involvement of central bank and had the fixed exchange rate whereas later on, followed the policy and approved the USD as their domestic currency while some of the European countries adopted Euro as common currency.

The Euro

In 1998, the European Central Bank also known as ECB with command from government officials established price stability in Germany (Frankfurt). Every member economy reserves a place on the ECB board. The new system offered more advantages for developing and smaller regions like Austria, Belgium and Netherlands to plan policy. Thus, the new arrangement started to operate in 1999 January. As within the tenure of three years, the Euro became the unit of account while not a medium of exchange. In this duration, the cost of liabilities, assets and commodity prices were calculated in Euro and local currency. The coins and notes of Euro started to circulate in 2002, ultimately substituting national currencies named as Italian Lira, French Franc or German Mark (Scott, 1998). The Euro, besides all non-member currencies, floated.

Summary

This chapter discusses the monetary system evolution from government and authorities-controlled coinage to fait money and then standards of golds, resulting in 'Bretton Woods system'. It also details the transformation from credit bills to fait money, which ultimately caused inflation and gold standards failure after WWI. The system named Bretton Woods came into existence in 1944 and nailed currencies to the US dollar with reserves of gold while in 1971 it collapsed. This resulted in floating exchange rated. In this chapter, the era of 1999 is covered emphasizing on introduction of Euro which later on replaced national currencies and assisted in stability of price. Lastly, modern monetary system along with currency, bank deposit, credit, electronic money, central banking and monetary theory are reviewed which explained their contribution in shaping global economies.

Learning Objectives

(1) To elaborate the evolution of money from the Middle Ages to the complex monetary systems of various currencies.
(2) To explain all the details related to the effects and development of monetary systems along with the future effects.
(3) To highlight the execution of operations and importance of money and banks.

Chapter 3

The Adoption of Internet in Financial Services

Introduction

The transition towards the usage of paper currency elevated the level of internationals trade considerably in Europe. Banks along with privileged group initiated currency buying from other economies and established the first market of currency. The stability of a specific government impacted the economy's currency worth and hence the ability of that economy to trade within the international market of currency.

Thus, the competition among economies usually direct to currency disputes, where competing economies might make effort to deviate the worth of the rival's currency via boosting the worth of currency and making the rivals goods costly or through reducing the worth of rival's product via devaluing the currency or imposing a ban on currency.

Whereas in the 21st century, the dynamics of economies started to change and move towards the rising trend of innovation. During this century, a unique mode of payment was introduced widely known as mobile payment. Through this unique mode of payment, bills can be paid, and it can be activated via a single touch. Also, this mode of payment offers benefits like money transfer, accessibility and convenience.

The usage of the internet within financial services is indeed a revolutionary phase in the history of finance. The considerable effect of the internet on the financial industry dates to its transformation from initial digital banking to the present innovation of fintech launch. This indicates an advancement of technology, changes with regulatory and changing preferences of customers which have initiated the integration of technology within the financial sector.

Online Banking Initiation

The initial kind of digital banking started in the 1960s when mainframe computers were introduced in banks to systematize banking features like assessing

The Global Evolution, Changing Landscape and Future of Financial Markets, 17–23
Copyright © 2025 Syed Ali Raza, Darakhshan Syed, Syed Rizwan and Maiyra Ahmed
Published under exclusive licence by Emerald Publishing Limited
doi:10.1108/978-1-83549-330-420251003

processing and the management of customer accounts (Nagaoka et al., 2005). In early 1980, banks began to provide services such as dial-up service to facilitate customer issues related to account from their home desktops.

Another service after dial-up was ATM which the Bank of America launched in 1960s, facilitating customer to withdraw money from their accounts without requiring to physically visit bank (Kaptan, 2002). Additionally, Citibank in 1980s launched the earliest system for online banking, which assists customers to check account details and execute banking transactions via dial-up service (Vidal, & Vidal-García, 2016).

Advancement in Online Banking

During the era of 1990s–2000s, portals for online banking were introduced to elevate the usage of internet (Vidal, & Vidal-García, 2016). Various banks created online-banking portals of their own banks to facilitate customers regarding account balance, transactions, payment of bills and money transfers from home desktops. Hence, internet banking/online-banking rapidly became a preferred option for the majority of population because of the accessibility.

For example, Stanford Federal Credit Union in 1994 was the first institution which introduced internet banking to its members, and Wells Fargo in 1996 launched internet-banking portals for their customers (Prodromou, 2020).

The evolution of banking in the 1990s saw the rise of internet banking, which transformed from a simple concept to a service used by millions of customers worldwide. Although internet banking was the outcome of varied generations of electronic transactions. The present internet-banking services are the result of various system generations like phone banking and automated teller machines (ATMs). ATMs were the earlier innovations offered to customers for electronic access while in phone banking, customers used to call their banking representative via ordinary phone and perform banking transactions via keypads. The online access of banking information through personal computers replaced phone banking and provided opportunity to customer to connect with banks via computers having a dial-up connection to phone. Personal computer banking involved maintenance expenditure for timely diverse modems and were considerably complicated installations.

Subsequent to those innovations, in 1996 Deutsche Bank introduced the first internet-banking plan in America along with Citibank, which launched a particular electronic toolkit in all branches of bank, globally (Grosse, 1997). Internet banking is based on the web browser connected to user interface, and for transfer of data, internet is essential as well as for downloads and hence considerably the cost of maintenance is reduced. For customers, internet banking provides recent information, 24/7 accessibility to banking services. The most important facilities offered by internet banking are money transfer, payment of bills and account balance can be checked. Other facilities like trading, mortgage payments and loans are included to these significant services.

According to Pew Research Centre in 2000, 17% of internet users had never used online-banking service while 32% users of internet used online-banking (Fox, 2013).

Additionally, in 1995, Fed processed around 49.5 billion cheques whereas in subsequent year (2000), Fed processed 42.5 billion cheques. Indicating a decline of 14% in the use of cheques, which means that people in that duration were gradually adopting the newly introduced service of internet banking (Wheelock, & Wilson, 2004).

Electronic Payment Advancements

Innovations involving electronic payments help to transfer funds via electronic means including less to no paperwork involved. Customers change their preference from cheques and cash to credit and debit cards, which are usually processed as well as cleared electronically. According to a report published by the Federal Reserve (2003), payment from credit card increase by 15 billion with an average of 7.3%, while transactions from debit card elevated to 8.3 billion, indicating growth of 35.6%, in 2000 (Belsky, & Essene, 2008). Based on the following estimates, highlighted the increasing preference of credit and debit card usage and declining rate of cheques and cash usage.

Likewise, during 1990 and 2000, the ratio of cash used for personal expenditure declined from 25.7% to 16.3% whereas the usage of cheque reduced from 61.8% to 56% (Hilgert et al., 2009). This served as an indicator reflecting the transition of customers from customary methods to electronic advancement which also served as a steppingstone towards accelerated use of ACH (automated clearing house). ACH serves as an alternate for regular payment via cheques like a direct depositor of payment, monthly mortgage payments withdrawals. ACH use was elevated due to the IT innovations which decreased expenditure and accelerated the accessibility and convenience of payment through electronic means.

During the era of 2000, internet banking was no longer a new phenomenon as people were shifting their preference from paper money to electronic system. The inclusion of internet banking facilitated customers by providing an online platform for trading which became much easier for customers to invest in financial instruments, stock and bonds across boarders through customers and investors gain advantage of diversification. In same era, Paypal also became widely popular due to its' convenience and security to perform online payments.

Like electronic mode of payments, mobile payments methods were introduced named Google wallet (changed to Google Pay) and endorsed by few financial institutions. Considering the wide acceptance of mobile payments, various other innovations like this were introduced under the label of digital wallets. These virtual wallets like Samsung Play and ApplePay, instituted the idea of utilizing smart phones for contactless payments and the payment information storage.

PayPal

PayPal was launched in 1990 to facilitate a payment system for the company named Confinity by Palm pilot users. But in 2000, the company was acquired by

X.com and later on became PayPal (Soni, 2022). This innovation was a mainstream payment mechanism for buyers and sellers of eBay. Further, in 2002 PayPal was acquired again by auction site and turned it into an official payment service. PayPal is a payment platform which can be accessed through websites and phone app which facilitates payment among parties via digital transfer of money. This advancement could be used by customers as well as by suppliers who accept PayPal. Suppliers could utilize PayPal card readers in physical stores or permit PayPal as an option for payment on website.

Customers make a payment of invoices as well as transferring money. Money could be transferred to any email/phone number; it is not necessary that recipient should have a PayPal account. An individual requires an email ID for account sign-up and needs to entire debit/credit card or instead should enter bank account information to complete the sign-up process. The next step includes verification by PayPal to ensure information is valid and the person is a rightful owner prior use of service.

Customers could select PayPal as an option to pay online for purchases made, but suppliers or retailers should have this service. Transactions through PayPal takes few minutes to be completed as well as company assure that transfers are offered for withdrawal and payment to a bank account promptly.

The use of PayPal within the business sector during 2000–2006 significantly contributed to the transition of digital and online payments. This platform ultimately became a considerably used and trusted financial service tool for businesses as well as for customers. The effect of this innovation on finance division was prominent during this duration, influencing the perspective of buyers and sellers performed transactions in the digital era.

Mobile Banking

Banking was further transferred to mobile as mobile financial transaction could be performed. By using mobile banking service, customers were able to execute numerous transactions at once. But earlier, mobile banking was introduced in the form of SMS or text and was known as SMS banking. Earlier, European banks were among the first few banks which were offering this service to their clients, as mobile banking facilities could be attained by mobile web through WAP support during 1999.

Initially, mobile web and banking through SMS were widely used services. But with the increasing use of smartphones as well as advancement, applications of mobile banking apps or applications started to transform. Customers can download banking apps onto their phones to get a refined interface along with enhanced capability to execute transactions.

Mobile banking is not just performing transaction via smartphones, but the service facilities are enormous. First, access to account information facilitates users to view balance and the statement of account online as well as pay with credit cards and other bills online. Second, the service to perform transactions helps customers to transfer funds as there is no need to visit a bank physically.

Third, through investment banking service, customers can manage portfolio as well as can access the real-time insight of their portfolio performance. Moreover, the ability to facilitate clients by support service assist users to view their status of request made for credit/loan and request for new card request.

However if mobile banking during the earlier is revisited, it is evident that the evolution of technology has transformed mobile banking immensely. For instance, in 1980, United American Bank with TRS-80 computers and modem was facilitating its users by providing home banking service. Following a similar path, other banks within the US started to experiment and revolutionize banking practices to gain customers.

In 1981, remote banking services were introduced in New York as renown banks like Chemical Bank, Citibank, Manufacturers Hanover and Chase Manhattan started to offer home banking services. While in 1983, the Bank of Scotland offered a service named 'Homelink' to officially provide internet banking to its customers within the UK. Bill payments and transfer of funds were performed via internet connection through phones and TVs (de la Torre et al., 2018).

Moving on, in 1994 Stanford Federal Credit Union as a financial institution offered online banking to its customers. Likewise, the Presidential Bank in 1995 was among the few initial banks which enabled customers to access account information online. During 1997, in the UK the Royal Bank of Scotland shifted internet banking service to text message (Howcroft et al., 2002).

As the banking sector analyzed the ongoing trend and potential of this service, banks started to persuade their users to use internet banking services through lucrative deals in form of discounts. By the end of 2006, around 80% of banks in the US had shifted banking services to internet platform (Wewege et al., 2020).

Tokenization

The integration of the internet in the financial sector was not just limited to ATMs, online banking and phone banking, but the advancement of technology was visible in other forms. As the virtual illustration of real-world assets from 1990s to present, various blockchains have been introduced. Another transformation in the financial sector during 1990s was tokenization, which was introduced as a novel advancement comparative to other investment options like mortgage and asset-backed securities (Hines, 2020). During the 1990s, tokenization in the financial sector was referred for security and e-payments (electronic payments).

The e-payments via tokenization in the same era of 1990s' process included replacing sensitive information such as the credit card number with a token, i.e. unique identifier. The replacement was introduced for security of e-transaction, particularly in card and online payment process. The entire process included several steps, initially when transaction by a credit card was performed by a customer, the credit card number could not be stored by the payment processor machine. But a unique identifier (token) that was randomly generated code was utilized instead of credit card number. Hence, this unique identifier was of no use to possible hackers as it was only useable within that payment system. Whereas the credit card actual number was safely saved via the transaction gateway.

The widely accepted phenomena of internet disseminated to various sectors which lead to a paradigm shift that ultimately changes the methods of operating businesses and paved the way for various issues and challenges for businesses, firms and industries to execute transactions via this novel distribution medium.

In the case of banking industry, this specific sector is a highly responsive sector which can build and increase its worth through internet advancement; therefore, various banks and financial institutes have transformed themselves from brick-mortar to click-mortar. Hence, to attain a competitive edge, the majority of banks adopted the innovation to provide novel experiences to their customers.

The internet of things (IoT) was advantageous for the financial sector and customers as the use of internet in the banking sector assist in cost reduction. The banks were able to operate with a smaller number of staff employed and a minimum number of branches due to internet banking. Second, due to internet banking, customers' costs and time were saved as the need to visit the bank was no longer needed, prompt response of queries was received. According to the US survey, around 15% of the year-on-year basis growth was observed during 2001–2006 regarding internet banking adoption (Lechman, 2013). Although the integration of the internet into customary practices posed various challenges and complexities for the financial sector and customers, the adoption rate of integrated financial services was widely accepted among both parties. Banking industry analysts evaluated the service's potential and prevailing trend. Banks began offering attractive incentives, such as discounts, to get customers to utilize their online banking services. Approximately, 80% of US banks have moved their banking services to online platforms by the end of 2006. Customers and the financial industry also benefited from the IoT since it reduced costs associated with internet use in banking. Thanks to internet banking, the banks were able to function with fewer employees and fewer locations. The second benefit of online banking is that it saves clients' money and time by eliminating the need to visit the bank and allowing for quick response to inquiries.

Summary

Europe's degree of international trade increased significantly when paper money became the norm. Banks and a select few started purchasing currency from other economies and created the first currency market. The stability of a particular government affected the value of the economy's currency and, consequently, the economy's capacity to transact on the global currency market. Initiated in the 1960s, digital banking took its first form. Banks started offering services like dial-up service in the beginning of 1980 to help customers with account-related problems from the comfort of their own homes. Online banking portals were established in the 1990s and 2000s to increase internet usage. A number of banks established their own online banking websites so that clients could access account information, make transactions, pay bills and transfer money from the comfort of their homes using desktop computers. Because of its accessibility, online banking and internet banking quickly gained popularity among most people. As more individuals shifted from using paper money to electronic systems, internet banking became commonplace around the year 2000.

Learning Objectives

(1) To introduce the need of mobile payment as a rising trend of innovation for financial services.
(2) To mention the initiation of online banking and other dial up facilities.
(3) To elaborate on the evolution and adaptation of online banking in the financial market.
(4) To describe the initial need and implementation of security mechanism in case of electronic payment.

Chapter 4

The Financial Crises and Money Market

The money market is an important part of the global financial system and at times may be a harbinger of financial crises and at other times a source of stability in the midst of crisis. The complex Web of the global financial system is intertwined with the money market. This chapter reviews the historical roots of major financial crises, the basics of the money market and the two concepts together. Understanding the basic causes of the major financial crises of modern time, the do's and don'ts when a financial crisis hits, and what regulatory policies towards financial institutions might do, are among the most important questions that any investor, policy-maker or financial institution stands to consider the answers of.

A Historical Overview of Major Financial Crises

The financial system periodically experiences sudden and severe disruption – financial crises that produce a somewhat grating and most un-melodic series of shocks and aftershocks to the economy around them. The money market, a crucial segment of the broader financial system, experiences those shocks right on its front lines – but how those aftershocks play out across the economy might not always be so clear.

The Great Depression

To understand the financial crisis, a retrospective of the Great Depression is in order. The Great Depression was a catastrophic economic event that sparked economic innovations in policy and thought. This crash course on the causes, context and consequences of the Great Depression is well worth a watch. Arguably, the most revealing context on the Great Depression was how the response to it revealed competing thoughts on economic policy.

Speculative excesses, bank panics and policy mistakes each contributed to the severity and duration of the Great Depression. The Depression offers lessons in the importance of credible, proactive policies, strong financial regulation and international coordination in preventing and ending financial crises.

The Global Evolution, Changing Landscape and Future of Financial Markets, 25–31
Copyright © 2025 Syed Ali Raza, Darakhshan Syed, Syed Rizwan and Maiyra Ahmed
Published under exclusive licence by Emerald Publishing Limited
doi:10.1108/978-1-83549-330-420251004

The 2008 Global Financial Crisis

In the grand scheme, the 2008 Global Financial Crisis looms as a watershed moment that precipitated sharp adjustments to the financial marketplace as well as subsequent regulatory frameworks. Originating from the seed money of the United States subprime mortgage market meltdown, the crisis rapidly escalated into a global catastrophe that severely impacted financial institutions, markets, and economies worldwide.

Behind the bubble, burgeoning complex financial instruments, lax risk management functions and zero regulatory oversight formed the recruiting class of the 2008 crisis, the resulting domino effect laying bare the broader cross-currents of global financial markets and the need for coordinated international efforts to moderate systemic risks.

Other Notable Financial Crises

The world economy has seen numerous financial crises apart from the Great Depression and 2008. The Asian Financial Crisis occurred in 1997, the Dot-Com Bubble Burst happened in the early 2000s and the European Sovereign Debt Crisis was witnessed in the aftermath of the 2008 downturn. Each one of these crises had its own unique characteristics, highlighting the need for a nuanced understanding of different economic contexts and drivers (Scott, n.d.).

Fundamentals of the Money Market

Definition and Functions

Before we move ahead, it is important to understand the basics. A money market is primarily made up of short-term, highly liquid instruments that provide a marketplace for the borrowing and lending of funds for brief periods. The money market performs the following functions:

- Providing liquidity.
- Providing for short-term borrowing and lending.
- Discovering a mechanism for call money and notice money interest rate.

Key Instruments of the Money Market

Some of the key instruments used by the money market players include Treasury bills, commercial paper, repurchase agreements and certificates of deposit. Together, these instruments form the lifeblood of this vital market, serving the varying needs of everyone from institutional investors to governments and financial institutions (Dodd, 2012).

The Role of Money Markets in Financial Stability

A sound and robust financial system would not exist without a stable money market. While it serves as a platform for short-term transactions, its significance extends to its role as a financial-system shock absorber, by which institutions facing funding pressures can liquefy assets.

Indeed, the money market's ability to swiftly accommodate shifts in supply and demand strengthens financial stability by mitigating disturbances and ensuring the efficient operation of the wider financial ecosystem.

Causes of Financial Crises

Financial crises stem from a variety of factors. By understanding these factors, it becomes easier to create measures to prevent them. Often, these causes boil down to economic imbalances, policy and regulatory shortfalls and the confluence of market psychology and investor behaviour.

Economic Factors

Economic imbalances such as excessive debt, inflation and asset bubbles can form the foundation for financial crises. The housing market bubble that burst, which was a key impetus for the 2008 crisis, was a product of imprudent lending practices and speculative excesses. Reform that works to recognize and address these imbalances is key to the prevention of crises.

Policy and Regulation Issues

The role of policy and regulatory frameworks in either attenuating or amplifying financial crises cannot be overstated. Inadequate oversight, weak regulatory standards and stuttering policy responses can all act to amplify the impact of economic shocks. The strengthening of regulatory frameworks and the consistent and accurate application of appropriate policy interventions are critical components of an effective preventative strategy.

Market Psychology and Investor Behaviour

The behavioural dimensions of market participants are central to the dynamics of financial crises. Herding, excessive risk-taking and irrational exuberance can combine to foster speculative bubbles and their subsequent implosions. Understanding and managing market psychology is central to nurturing a more stable and resilient financial environment (Scott et al., 2021).

Impact of Financial Crises on the Money Market

Short-Term Funding and Liquidity Concerns

During financial crises, money market related activities can be stricken by worries about short-term funding and liquidity. As existential concern about an institution heightens, the ability to access short-term funding can be diminished, thus disrupting normal money market functioning. Tamping down any liquidity scares is a fundamental facet of crisis management.

Interest Rate Volatility

Interest rates are often very volatile as a result of financial crises and serve as a primary factor impacting money market dynamics. In an effort to stabilize markets, central banks may alter interest rates, but the resulting fluctuations can impact money market lending and borrowing expectations. Understanding what is happening with interest rates is vital for money market participants moving through uncertain times.

Effects on Financial Institutions and Investors

Financial crises ripple beyond borrowers and lenders. Participation in the money market means banks and nonbanks bear the weight of financial crises. And they may face solvency and liquidity challenges that require intervention. Credit lines, in the form of guarantees and swaps, provide financial assistance to financial institutions. Additionally, policy measures may involve central banks, government treasuries and deposit insurance companies stepping in until panic abates.

At the same time, investors must navigate in a cloud of uncertainty. As the overall level of default increases, it becomes increasingly difficult to ascertain counterparty risk. In response to such increased uncertainty many investors choose to deleverage or exit the market. In trembling from the crisis, investor portfolios begin to topple. And with investor flight, financial institutions liquidate their assets. Or, in a rather insouciant manner, ratings agencies downgrade them from investment grade to junk status. In an effort to minimize expected losses, investors reassess relative risk exposures and their investment strategies ('The Global Financial Crisis | Explainer | Education | RBA', n.d.).

Policy Responses to Financial Crises

Ensuring a robust response to financial crises is crucial for minimizing their impact. Think of it this way: when these crises hit, it's like a coordinated effort where central banks, governments and regulatory authorities step up to the plate. They become the superheroes in this financial saga, working together to put various measures into action. Their mission? To bring back stability and confidence in the financial world, providing a sense of security during challenging times.

Just like a team of skilled professionals, they each bring their unique strengths to the table, aiming to safeguard the well-being of the global economy.

Central Bank Interventions

Central banks have many tools to intervene in the money market and the broader financial system. These tools include adjusting interest rates, open market operations and extraordinary measures such as quantitative easing. The effectiveness of central bank interventions depends on their ability to restore confidence, provide liquidity and address systemic vulnerabilities.

Government Fiscal Policies

Governments often implement fiscal policies to counteract the negative effects of financial crises. Stimulus packages, infrastructure spending and tax measures are common tools of economic activity. Balancing short-term relief with long-term fiscal sustainability is a delicate task for policymakers grappling with crises.

Regulatory Reforms and Measures

Post-crisis, regulatory reforms come to the forefront. The aim is to protect the financial system against future shocks. Risk management practices are enhanced. Regulatory oversight is channelled up.

At the same time, measures to guarantee transparency and to contribute to a global information exchange are struck. Our agenda asserts that these changes balance the demand for innovation and that they also take aim at the preservation of stability ('Policy Responses to the Global Financial Crisis (Financial Economics)' 2021).

Case Studies: Money Market Stress During Financial Crises

Money Market Mutual Funds (MMFs): A Financial Stability Case Study

During the 2008 financial crisis, Money Market Mutual Funds (MMFs) were subjected to a critical test of their financial stability. Despite being marketed as safe investment vehicles governed by Securities and Exchange Commission (SEC) Rule 2a-7, MMFs were exposed as susceptible to runs. The share price of the Reserve Primary Fund 'broke the buck' and fell from \$1.00 to \$0.97, sparking heavy redemptions and creating a run dynamic that threatened the broader financial system.

Analysis of Specific Events and Responses

Policymakers took steps in response. The Treasury Department provided temporary deposit insurance, while the Federal Reserve set up emergency facilities. SEC reforms included it allowing – and, over time, mandating – a shift to floating net asset values (NAVs) for prime and municipal MMFs and assessing their vulnerability under hypothetical scenarios in stress testing.

Reforms have remade the MMF landscape, fostering the growth of government MMFs and a contraction of institutional prime and institutional municipal MMFs. Ongoing policy debate concerns whether MMFs' NAV is stable enough. Advocates of a floating NAV emphasize that it eliminates the incentive for runs (Su, 2020).

Lessons Learnt and Preventive Strategies

Adaptive regulatory frameworks became a necessity following the financial crisis as policymakers realized that a dynamic financial landscape cannot be managed effectively with a one-size-fits-all approach. The SEC's multi-year process of reforming Rule 2a-7 demonstrates the critical role that ongoing evaluation and adjustments play in mitigating systemic risks associated with MMFs.

Risk Management Practices

Stress testing is now a critical practice for preventing a market run. MMFs are required today to assess their ability to withstand a variety of hypothetical scenarios. Whether it's through the Dodd-Frank stress tests for asset managers or the new SEC mandated stress tests for MMFs, the industry is committed to proactively managing risks.

Regulatory and Supervisory Enhancements

Ongoing policy debates about the balance between financial market stability and market discipline will ground much of this activity. This has been a dynamic marketplace and the industry's ability to adapt is perhaps no more evident than the move to a floating NAV for Institutional Prime MMFs and Institutional Municipal MMFs. The ongoing assessment of the impact of the reforms caused Representative Carolyn Maloney (D-NY), along with others to introduce the Consumer Financial Choice and Capital Markets Protection Act of 2019 ('Money Market Mutual Funds: A Financial Stability Case Study' 2019).

The Future of Financial Crises and Money Markets

Predictions and Preparedness Strategies

The future of financial crises in the coming years is an especially challenging problem to solve. Rapidly advancing technology, changing geopolitical factors and more integrated financial systems make predicting financial crises more difficult. The work of identifying and managing risk, and being prepared, is critical. The rapid growth of financial technology and digitization has ushered in an era of new capabilities and risks to the financial sector. Both brought to light by the financial crisis, the global marketplace now is tied together in a way that it was not before.

The increasing risks to the financial sector and global economy due to technological failures and cyber threats are highlighted, along with the initial indications that an adequate regulatory framework for fintech has been established. This framework aims to balance the political push for significant financial deregulation with the demand for innovative financial services technologies. It also addresses the need to prepare for potential future financial crises driven by fintech developments (Nanto, 2009).

Summary

The relationship between financial crises and the money market requires comprehensive knowledge of historical antecedents, core principles and evolving dynamics. As we confront this uncertainty, our goal must be to advance a path characterized by the lessons of past crises, the solid risk management that is the cornerstone of any company and a dynamic process of upticks in the soundness of global financial systems.

Fostering such resilience will rely on the combined efforts of policymakers, regulators and market participants. This endeavour will call for a strategy that embodies an openness to the vagaries of economic change, a temperate approach to technological advances and an eager embrace of collaboration across borders.

Learning Objectives

(1) Recognize financial crises and its numerous origins and triggers, as well as their historical background.
(2) Examine the build-up, burst-bubble and spreading effects of a financial crisis.
(3) Examine the effects of significant financial crises, including the global financial crisis, the Asian financial crisis, the Great Depression and the Oil Crisis.
(4) Recognize how money markets work, how they behave in times of crisis and why reform and regulation are necessary in order to preserve financial stability.
(5) Determine the insights that may be drawn from previous crises and crisis management techniques, such as risk management procedures, legislative changes and the changing dynamics of the cryptocurrency and digital marketplaces.
(6) Elucidate the insights gained from previous crises and crisis management approaches, encompassing risk mitigation techniques, regulatory modifications and the dynamic terrain of digital and cryptocurrency exchanges.
(7) Analyze the development of fintech, the rise of artificial intelligence (AI) and the shift in the financial markets towards AI-driven finance.

Chapter 5

Trends of AI in Financial Services and Its Applications

Introduction

There is no questioning that technology has had a significant impact on how individuals live. Everything has gone digital, including the way people interact and manage finances. As early customers of online banking programs and budgeting tools, financial services have been at the forefront of this digital revolution. It therefore comes as no surprise that this trend will continue to grow in the upcoming years. The banking sector will be significantly impacted by artificial intelligence (AI). AI is currently being utilized in various fields such as fraud detection, financial advice, investment management and simplified customer service. Furthermore, when AI develops further, we should anticipate seeing even more cutting-edge financial applications. AI might be used, for instance, to automate insurance claims processing or build individualized investment portfolios.

AI and Its Importance

AI is the potential of technology, especially computer systems that approximate human intellect's functions. Some specialized applications of AI include natural language processing, automated speech recognition, intelligent systems and machine learning (ML). Typically, AI systems work by ingesting enormous amounts of labelled training data, looking for patterns and relationships in the data and then extrapolating future state estimations from these patterns. By analyzing millions of instances, an image recognition initiative can gain the ability to recognize and explain items in photos, and a chatbot fed samples of text may develop the ability to create realistic conversations with individuals. Realistic text, images, music and other media can be produced with new and rapidly developing generative AI algorithms.

The potential for AI to change how humans perform routine tasks, entertain others and approach life makes it important. It has been effectively implemented

The Global Evolution, Changing Landscape and Future of Financial Markets, 33–46
Copyright © 2025 Syed Ali Raza, Darakhshan Syed, Syed Rizwan and Maiyra Ahmed
Published under exclusive licence by Emerald Publishing Limited
doi:10.1108/978-1-83549-330-420251005

in business to automate labour-intensive human tasks, such as quality control, fraud detection, lead generation and customer care. AI does several activities significantly more effectively than humans. AI systems often do tasks quickly and with minimal error, particularly in repeated, detail-oriented tasks like reviewing a large volume of court documents to ensure crucial fields are correctly completed. Owing to its enormous data handling capacity, AI can offer firms previously undiscovered insights into their operations. The significance of AI and its ensuing elements have been extensively recognized. They are viewed as techniques and tools used to improve the world. These devices are valuable and helpful tools that expedite your tasks and processes with proven accuracy and precision. These innovations and applications are not limited to improving the world's error-free state through common sense methods; they also connect to areas beyond an individual's daily lives. It affects and is significant for other fields as well.

AI in Financial Services

AI in finance refers to the application of technology, such as ML, to improve financial organizations' analysis, management, investment and money-protection processes by simulating human intellect and decision-making. The banking sector, when compared to other businesses, has demonstrated itself as a pioneering user of AI. This illustrates the plethora of uses of AI and ML in the finance industry. In some way, these applications may be extremely known to financiers, insurance companies, investors and investment managers. To get a competitive advantage in the marketplace, forward-thinking entrepreneurs and upper management professionals actively investigate new applications of AI in finance.

The application of AI in financial services has a significant impact on the industry's main company structures and competitive status. The most prominent of these changes is the propensity of AI algorithms to display a 'flywheel' impact, which favours early adopters and may create obstacles to entrance. The term 'AI-flywheel' refers to the propensity of AI models to show self-reinforcing economies of scale, in which a more accurate model draws in more users and data, both of which improve the accuracy of the model. The financial service industry will see a paradigm shift in how businesses create profitable business models as a result of this flywheel effect, which will make granular data flows more crucial and raise the possibility of 'winner-take-all' behaviours. A lot of the new AI-powered enterprises focus on redefining their client experience, enabling customers manage their own financial matters and serving as a reliable resource when they need it. Banking organizations are laying the foundation for 'self-driving finance,' that's going to upend current competitive dynamics and eventually bring rewards to the owner of the consumer experience, as they continue to apply AI to client advise and interactions. The imperative to swiftly obtain novel proficiencies could have contributed to the heightened curiosity of established financial establishments to establish collaborations with FinTech firms, which they before seen as possible rivals. Both of these organizations stand to benefit from these agreements when they succeed. FinTechs can rely on the established credibility and clientele of existing financial service organizations, while incumbent firms can benefit from FinTechs' technological proficiency. According to the literature, one of the main factors influencing AI's overall effects will be its effect on the competitive landscape.

Financial service businesses will compete to be the first to use AI technology, to hire the best AI personnel and to produce the greatest value as it develops. The talents needed by financial institutions have changed due to the innovations spearheaded by this small group of employees. Organizations may become leaner as back-office procedures are streamlined. The vocations that don't require specialized training or abilities have the highest likelihood of being automated. Routine low- and middle-complexity occupations will be significantly impacted by the growing usage of AI. Net job losses are inevitable, nevertheless, as these positions make up a sizeable portion of the Financial Services sector's employment.

The Rise of AI in the Financial Sector

The latest developments in AI have caught the interest of experts and stock market analysts. Although artificial neural networks have the potential to dynamically decide any nonlinear expression with a suitable number of hidden components, they are one of the most attractive models utilized by experts in analyzing and predicting the direction of stock market trend. Experts and stock market participants are interested in the latest advancements in AI. Artificial neural networks are one of the most popular models used by specialists in stock estimation and prediction despite their ability to dynamically determine any nonlinear expression with an appropriate number of hidden components. Banks, insurance companies, financial institutions and other industries employ predictive analytics. Predictive analytics may provide a more accurate future picture by providing data directly to the management team, saving time and effort for every department. Financial institutions are implementing AI at an astonishing rate since individuals make mistakes more frequently. Activities that require a lot of resources repeatedly work effectively with AI programs.

Financial companies may now speed and automate tedious, manual activities like market research by utilizing AI. Investors may monitor the growth of their investments and evaluate risk by identifying patterns and forecasting future performance, thanks to AI's quick processing of enormous data sets. Since personal data may be gathered and used to determine prices and coverage, inspection is also relevant to insurance. AI is helpful in cybersecurity as well, especially when it comes to identifying fraudulent transactions. AI can recognize anomalous activity, instantly alert the institution and the customer to verify the purchase or transfer and, if required, take corrective action by continuously monitoring purchase behaviour and comparing it to historical data.

The whole client's experience in banking could potentially be improved with AI and ML. The emergence of online banking, often referred to as contactless banking, lessens the need for in-person interactions; yet this shift to virtual communications could result in a rise in endpoint vulnerabilities (e.g. smartphones, PCs and mobile devices). AI can automate a wide range of standard banking operations, such as payments, cash deposits, transfers and customer support queries. AI can also handle the almost rapid approval and rejection of mortgage and credit card application processes.

Advantages of AI in the Financial Sector

AI can speed up processes and techniques, work autonomously and effectively and enhance decision-making and the provision of services. AI can help payments providers automate cybersecurity procedures, for example, by continuously observing and analyzing network data. Alternatively, it could reinforce a bank's client-first approach by providing more customized, flexible digital banking solutions that meet and protect customer needs. AI can help financial services organizations manage human errors in processing information, statistical analysis, document processing and onboarding, customer interactions and other processes with automated software algorithms that follow consistent protocols.

In addition to processing information faster than a person, AI can recognize links and patterns in data that a human might overlook. Faster insights to support trading interactions, management of compliance, risk training, decision-making and other processes will result from this. AI can be used to assist clients with financial activities, goal-oriented problem-solving and financial management and control from any location. AI and ML can work continually on their designated tasks when operating in the cloud. Swiftly analyzing large volumes of data can result in novel and inventive offerings of goods and services that outperform the competition. Predictive analytics is one area where AI has been applied to modernize insurance client interactions while retaining a human element.

Trends of AI in Financial Services

Financial services and banks have undergone significant development. Branches no longer handle nearly as much traffic as they formerly did. With the advent of new payment methods, cash usage has decreased. Native rivals have entered the game, including well-funded biotech's and innovative startups.

All organizations are once more on the cusp of a revolutionary shift in their current state. There is a generational explosion of opportunity due to the rapid growth of AI, cloud computing and data processing and storage. Many bankers have the same sense of wonder that their colleagues had 25 years ago as we approach the Age of AI. In the end, banking is a bit-by-bit operation based on a decade-long trust guarantee. Applying AI in every aspect of it is made possible by a business strategy that is essentially digital at its core. Though they won't alter the core principles of banking, these technologies will fundamentally alter nearly every component of its operations.

Improved Consumers' Decision-Making Regarding Finances

The two main functions of banks are to grant loans and take deposits. Lending was traditionally limited to homeowners, and credit organizations relied on making loans. One type of consumer credit contract is a loan; banks own loans because they make money from the interest that borrowers pay back over the course of lengthy agreements. Thus, before making a loan offer, banks evaluate their finances and other pertinent data to decide whether to approve the loan and what the terms of repayment will be. A bank's success depends on its ability to accurately choose which customers to lend to minimize risk and optimize the typically low revenue margins of retail banking. Businesses nowadays are mostly digital and dynamic. Consequently, this transition is advantageous to businesses. Since people are affected by organizations' capacities to collect, analyze, manipulate and utilize data, modern firms are built on it. Numerous web-based platforms offer channels for gathering information. In addition, the capacity to convert the gathered data into value for financial benefit is inventive as is typical of the contemporary entrepreneur. True information is found in an organization's capacity to generate actionable insight and use it to inform more thoughtful and strategic decisions. Financial organizations should make better decisions by connecting them to the impact they hope to achieve.

AI possesses the ability to completely change the process of making financial decisions. By employing ML algorithms AI can analyze large volumes of data and deliver findings that humans are unlikely to notice. Making forecasts based on past data is one of the key advantages of utilizing AI in financial decision-making. By recognizing developments and patterns in financial markets, ML algorithms enable traders and investors to make better-informed selections.

Big data analytics is an all-encompassing approach to gathering, applying and evaluating massive and heterogeneous datasets with the goal of uncovering hidden patterns, unknown connections, trends in the marketplace and consumer demands that can help businesses make more educated and effective business decisions. Big data analytics, as an improved framework for gathering, transforming and organizing unstructured data into databases, may identify corporate growth prospects in both new and established enterprises, forecast consumer behaviour and help companies make smarter, more strategic business decisions. Big data analytics can process, evaluate and turn data into value while enhancing decision-making for the good of enterprises. Big data analytics has a great deal of potential to benefit businesses, especially when it is correctly matched with knowledge requirements and business cycles. Big data analytics has the potential to improve business activities performance by assisting organizations in anticipating unforeseen circumstances and enhancing their performance process through cost savings, optimal operation strategies, reduced inventory levels, highly productive workforces and elimination of waste. Big data analytics is essential for making business decisions and can provide companies with a competitive edge. Big data analytics can also impact organizational performance and the efficacy of operations processes. Entrepreneurs may improve marketing tactics and revenue strategy, as well as anticipate consumer patterns and preferences, by leveraging big data analytics.

ML techniques, deep learning and unsupervised clustering have become the preferred methods for developing applications that understand customer preferences and suggest new goods or services that they would enjoy. Recommendation engines are common ML systems that match customers with services they have enjoyed in the past or would want in the future. By discovering the finest possibilities for users to search systems, these recommendations relieve users of some of their mental weight. In a similar vein, AI can assist in forecasting conversion rates and customer lifetime values. AI can anticipate a user's future value or ascertain the likelihood that a consumer will purchase the premium edition of a product based on trends and historical consumer behaviour data collected during the product's testing stage.

Elimination of Silos to Improve Customer Experience

The traditional operating patterns of banks make it more difficult for them to meet the demand for constant innovation. Most standard banks are set up as cost centres with centralized teams for technology and analytics and discrete business lines. Owners of businesses set their own goals, and when they do, they frequently do so in a way that is insufficient or weak in relation to the enterprise's technology and analytics plan. Working groups with silos and 'waterfall' implementation techniques almost always result in delays, spending excessively and less-than-ideal performance. Organizations also lack strong chains of feedback and a test-and-learn mentality, which are essential for quick experimentation and incremental progress. Business executives, frequently dissatisfied with the results of previous initiatives and trials, have a tendency to depend on outside technology suppliers for essential functions, starving their own teams of expertise and capabilities that should ideally be created internally to ensure competitive difference.

Large volumes of unstructured data can be rapidly standardized by NLP and turned into valuable knowledge. The client experience is another advantage for financial services organizations that are greatly impacted by AI. Chatbots, or digital assistants that converse with clients via text message or voice commands, are one method AI might enhance this crucial aspect of conducting business. They can be configured to provide tailored recommendations in addition to providing answers to frequently asked inquiries concerning goods and services. The bank's data management must provide data availability or the ability to access, take in and interact with the data that serve as the foundation for all insights and decisions made at the decision-making layer. Data liquidity increases and more divisions can collaborate more effectively when functional silos are removed. The initial phase in the data value chain is the constant sourcing of facts from all relevant external sources and internal systems. To do this, data must be ingested into a reservoir, cleaned and labelled as needed for different use cases, and incoming data must be separated from that of existing and potential clients so that data that can be analyzed immediately may be separated from data that has to be cleaned and tagged for later use.

AI is expected to become popular in a domain where a lot of customers complain: the overwhelming phone tree they encounter when contacting their financial institution. Now, the customers won't need to go through selections or wait to speak with a representative when using chatbots; the bot will take responsibility for the customer's query straight away. Based on this current trend, it is anticipated that these chatbots will revolutionize the way customers are served. Consumers will only need to ask the bot on the other end of the line for account information or personal inquiries instead of calling their bank. Customers have been interacting with brands and companies they support more through messaging applications than through social network ones. This indicates that businesses need to change and figure out how to allow text messaging if they want to stay up to date with technology and draw in this new wave of digital natives. Banks can break down organizational silos, improve goal and priority alignment throughout the organization and increase responsiveness and efficiency by combining business and technology into collaboratively owned platforms managed by multidisciplinary teams.

Increased Access to Real-Time Monetary Statistics

Computational finance was first introduced in the early 1990s and concentrated on using AI to make investment decisions in the stock market. Now, it covers three main areas of finance: sentiment analysis of articles or social media posts regarding the businesses or resources, economic portfolio optimization and upcoming pricing or trend forecasting in financial investments. The ability to identify and investigate patterns that humans fail to consider, the ability to consume information instantly in real-time and the omission of instantaneous irrationality brought on by emotional decision-making are the key benefits of using computational techniques to robotize the financial investment procedures. Researchers on the field of digital finance have also been conducted in the areas of network inspection, trading behaviour analysis, agglomeration of financial resources and management of complex systems applied to the financial sector. The predictions were made using statistical techniques at first, but in more recent times, AI systems have taken over. Scholars and traders are increasingly employing historical time series for stock market prediction or forecasting to make financial gains from stock trading. Another advantage of the of being gathered by fintech businesses is the enhancement of notifications and tracking for financial transactions.

The way fraud is now managed can lag in real-time because of data silos and a lack of transaction visibility; this technology can help overcome these issues. With increasing power, AI systems will be able to detect suspect activities or money laundering before it's too late, as opposed to after the fact. This technology also has the potential to assist banks in identifying anomalies before they become serious issues.

Robotic and Cognitive Automation (R-CA)

The term R-CA describes a wide range of technological features, from AI and cognitive automation to robots that duplicate human behaviour and intelligence. Robotic process automation (RPA) is one of the various technologies that allow basic task automation. Although it has been around for a while, it has improved, escalated and become more affordable within the last 10 years. A decade ago, a lot of automation systems and suppliers were still in their beginnings and had difficulty surviving the rigorous examination of IT security inspections. They have the governance, security and infrastructure to handle enterprise programs today, and they are well-established. Also, compared to earlier generations of technologies, modern task-automation solutions are simpler to implement and use. A finance professional can now be trained to create a large portion of the RPA workflow, when previously a manager would have to wait for an overworked IT team to install a bot.

Financial services can achieve cost savings of 20–60% of baseline FTE expenses with the use of RPA, according to Ernst & Young (Ordemann, 2017). Finance and accounting departments can drastically change how they carry out their everyday tasks by cutting expenses, improving accuracy and executing business procedures rapidly. The experts in the accounting and finance areas may now devote more of their efforts to high value, planned and consultancy jobs that support businesses' continued profitability, innovation and competitiveness because of this emerging trend.

Automating tasks requiring perception or evaluation are made feasible by the combination of cognitive technology with RPA. Incorporating natural language processing, chatbots, speech recognition and computer vision technologies, for example, enables bots to extract and organize data from text, photos, speech or audio and forward that organized data to the subsequent stage of the procedure. As an additional illustration, ML can help RPA prioritize tasks by spotting trends and forecasting process results. Beyond simple automation, Robotic and Cognitive Automatic (R-CA) can produce corporate results like increased client satisfaction, decreased turnover and higher revenue. To automate the billing procedure and stop income leakage caused by discrepancies between account cards and customer invoices, a US bank implemented R-CA. Client agreements and bills were in various dialects and on document either as PDFs or printed versions. This presented several issues for typical bots, including the labour-intensive and error-prone nature of manual documentation validation. In order to detect billing alternatives and fails, the bank used methods based on natural language processing to scan charge schedules and payments and interpret the process demands into an automated, operational business process execution.

Businesses have been comparatively slow to adopt cognitive process automation applications even though many major enterprise software companies have started to include cognitive technologies into their services and that applications powered by ML that give organizations more insight are multiplying. This is due to the complexity and scarcity of expertise needed to design and develop bespoke solutions based on cognitive technology. The increasing market for RPA is probably going to accelerate the adoption of cognitive automation as businesses move from RPA to additional cognitive technologies for their robotics operations.

Using RPA platforms to deploy cognitive technology could provide advantages over internal development or infrastructure expenditures such as faster installation with less work and a quicker return on investment. Several things came to consideration:

- Consider the possibility of cognitive improvements when using RPA. Cognitive RPA can expand the range of automation possibilities in addition to improving back-office automation.
- Businesses that use RPA typically concentrate on ways to remove jobs. However, they might also be able to expand their business and deal with demand spikes more skillfully. The application of cognitive RPA may offer chances to reorganize workforces and transfer employees to higher-value positions, such as those involving problem-solving and customer interaction.

R-CA is a concept that many organizations are just recently beginning to investigate. They would gain by adopting a strategic viewpoint as they proceed. Bots are capable of much more than just automating mundane tasks. RPA has the potential to be a cornerstone of initiatives aimed at leveraging cognitive technology and digitizing corporations.

AI-Driven Services for Brokerages

AI is gathering a lot of information on an individual's purchasing and selling patterns in the real estate industry, since the quantity of advertisements increases by thousands every hour. By doing this, the AI algorithms are being further adjusted to match the appropriate homeowners and investors. Most of the time this is accomplished without the need for intermediaries.

Despite this, the agents have been utilizing AI in unconventional manners. AI has been widely used to gather client leads and separate serious purchasers from casual browsers. They can offer buyers a wider range of options, thanks to AI. Because of this, both the agents and the clients benefit from the application of AI.

Robo-advisers are one application of AI in the financial advising industry. Robo-advisor is software that can offer limited financial advice and select equities for portfolios based on the client's preferred balance. Like other expert systems, robot-advisors duplicate the decision-making and actions of a seasoned human with specific expertise in each sector by employing AI technologies coupled with a knowledge base. These agents solve frequently asked easy queries and forward the complex ones to the human advisors in that way it makes the application highly responsive and at the same time reduces cost.

Security and Authentication

In the modern world, banking security is a major concern. One of the things that is mandatory to be considered is an attack on the organization's cybersecurity. These flaws in security lead to fraud and other malpractices. The number of people falling prey to bank fraud is increasing annually. Reducing the frequency and impact of credit catastrophes that harm the economy is the aim of financial security net initiatives. Threat financing companies often partnered with non-investing parties, regardless of whether they were state-sponsored or privatized. Technology, networks and systems must be protected from unauthorized access with security and authentication. To stay ahead of possible cyberattacks and develop effective countermeasures, the financial sector needs an exclusive cybersecurity team in a modern technologically evolved environment. Data security, computer safety mobile security, antivirus software, secure payment, online user confidentiality, security padlocks and a particular worldwide shield are all considered to be major components of cybersecurity.

Secure payment processing is essential to data security and authentication for any organization that handles online payments or transactions. They are encouraged to remain up to date on the latest advancements in e-commerce and secure transaction techniques and seek advice on how to incorporate them into their operations. AI-based cyber security solutions have been implemented to impose higher levels of protection. Every logged real-time information and notification is flagged by AI's spam screening for unsuitable material. Because malware can adapt and acquire knowledge, it can be identified. Consumers are advised not to open any correspondence that contains this dangerous software since it is instantly identifiable. Businesses can use folder security to safeguard their software applications and platform operations by utilizing data stacking, deactivation and file backups. Other alternatives include critical control, biometric authentication, encoding and cryptography. Network security aims to prevent a variety of harmful threats from entering or propagating within a network and hence safeguarding the architecture of financial institutions. This can be achieved through a variety of strategies. Big data, statistics, ML and AI are some of the approaches used in behavioural analysis. Behaviour analysis is a field within the natural sciences that focuses on the behaviour of individuals. Behavioural analysts strive to comprehend how an individual's or a creature's biological processes, pharmacology and surroundings influence their conduct. ML is used by a subset of business intelligence (BI) to find new patterns, connections and discoveries. A large portion of the work that data analysts typically do is automated using AI.

AI is also used to evaluate the likelihood of default of applicants for consumer and small business loans. The software makes use of algorithms and financial information to recognize trends and classify applications as good or bad. The technique of predictive analytics focuses on the most efficient techniques to conduct business operations and sales to detect unauthorized activity. Structured and unstructured data analysis can reveal hidden relationships that ultimately help the financial sector.

Generative AI (GenAI) in Finance

The latest AI based trend introduced in 2023 for boosting the financial services to a considerable extent is termed as Generative AI (GenAI) (McKinsey & Company, 2023). This is a stronger form of AI. GenAI has the strength to shape multiple areas of financial companies in a better way. GenAI basically utilizes ML-based techniques that provide reliable predictions by identifying association rules and hidden patterns from the collected information. GenAI provides results that are more accurate and optimized by addressing incomplete, inconsistent and noisy real time information.

GenAI performs smart data analysis to optimize costs and improve operational efficiency of the financial sector while minimizing the chances of human generated errors and optimizing automated tasks at the same time. It also enables the financial sector to deal with big data altogether, which was not possible with past AI techniques. The big data analytics generated by GenAI facilitates the organization to develop improved risk mitigation plans, detect fraudulent activities more accurately and make decisions in case of investments.

Recently, there has been a noticeable increase in demand for AI innovation in the banking sector because of mostly the user-friendly and automatic appearance of GenAI tools, as well as the arrival of digital content-generating features. The full end-to-end automation of financial markets by AI is still mostly in the research and development stage. However, if AI is used more widely, it may increase markets' inherent risks and create new difficulties.

Applications of AI in Financial Services

Commercial financial institutions use AI in all their main business departments. Using traditionally unutilized data types, AI can be applied to lending to generate precise forecasts. It is possible to enhance profitability, support prospective customers and improve predictive models of credit risk by examining these underutilized data sources. The handling of payments may be safer for clients by utilizing AI to identify money laundering and fraudulent transactions. Additionally, branch networks and ATMs can save operating expenses by using AI to forecast cash demand. Banks can identify suspect activity within their staff, report suspicious client operations and deal with the growing number of rules rapidly by utilizing AI in compliance.

AI can assist in more precise customer selection and product recommendations for customers in both sales and marketing. AI can help financial institutions in the investment and administration of accounts by lowering the cost of cash deposits and offering new products and services to individuals. Financial institutions stand to gain greatly from these ubiquitous AI applications in the future but only if several obstacles are handled. Higher profitability can result from better risk management when utilizing AI, if comprehensibility is guaranteed, and the ML techniques are documented in a manner that satisfies regulatory standards. AI has the potential to improve business and regulatory compliance effectiveness but only if the privacy issue in the context of AI is addressed. The banking institution's expenses can be decreased by more effectively managing the business infrastructures but only if AI can be incorporated into the operational procedures.

Alibaba and Jingdong use AI to extend loans to merchants and individuals ahead of time. Collateral guarantees are not required of lenders, and the entire operation cycle can be watched over by the background. The platform thoroughly and successfully analyzes customers' requirements, resources, financial status, actions and other criteria before traders request loans, and a client access whitelist is created. Simultaneously, it creates a pre-credit framework based on its risk tolerance and proactively establishes a pre-credit limit for consumers that may be dynamically altered at various points in response to shifting demand and various scenarios. Its supply chain finance division has achieved real-time credit limit conversion, uniform credit extension and closed-loop supervision of the overall association. The stock exchange is growing in scale and quantity of participants, with a relatively significant number of financiers. The public is becoming increasingly aware of AI-based frameworks because of market requirements.

Smart risk control using neural networks, knowledge visuals, ML, data inquiry and other technical structures, combined with background information for customer surveys, financing evaluation, lending authorization and credit approval after credit collection, significantly increases the effectiveness of each process and enhances the customer satisfaction level. To improve accuracy during usage, the model is iterated repeatedly based on user response. AI technologies process multi-dimensional organized and unorganized facts, analyze and filter suspicious activities and gain knowledge from previous cases to increase the effectiveness of anti-fraud and anti-money laundering efforts.

AI and big data technologies are used in marketing to analyze and categorize user-generated data. The platform combines relevant information, including purchasing inclinations, financial condition and behavioural patterns, to precisely position customers' demands, create customer profiles, anticipate client demands, match and push customized items and create marketing copy. Advertisers and companies are gradually realizing the benefits of smart marketing, and they have invested in a variety of industries to create a well-developed infrastructure.

Future of AI and the Financial Services Industry

The banking industry has extended its reach into the sales, information technology and telecommunication sectors to deliver solutions like smartphone banking, online banking and real-time financial transactions to satisfy client expectations. Customers can always access banking because of these cutting-edge capabilities, but the banking sector suffers a price for them. The involvement of telecommunications, sales and infotech has raised the likelihood of sending private data across virtual networks. It occasionally results in fraud and cyberattacks in the banking industry. This type of fraud damages the bank not just financially but also in terms of public trust.

AI's main objective in the banking sector is to help customers by giving their options priority. AI also contributes to ensuring that customers are satisfied with the services provided by the bank. AI aids the bank in comprehending customer expectations.

AI will support the expansion of financial services. Numerous companies have embraced digital transformation, gaining new insights into their data, increasing productivity and selling. They will have to scale up the personalization of relationship-based engagement with customers in the future. AI is crucial in facilitating customized customer service, generating safer and more responsible goods and assistance suggestions and building trust by expanding the range of service options that are offered at the most convenient times for clients.

Financial companies will also need to create robust and distinctive permission-based electronic client profiles; nonetheless, the information they require can be stored in separate silos. Financial institutions may design solutions that effectively scale while catering to the specific demands of their customers by dismantling these barriers, implementing an AI layer and utilizing human interaction in an effortless manner.

Summary

AI becomes important because technology can transform how people proceed in their daily lives, entertain others and complete everyday activities. Automation of labour-intensive human operations, such quality supervision, fraud detection, generating leads and customer service, has been successfully adopted in business. AI has a significant contribution in the financial services by providing smart highly responsive applications and predictions for stakeholders. In contrast to other industries, the banking sector has demonstrated to be innovative in the implementation of AI. This demonstrates the wide range of applications of AI and ML in the finance sector.

AI utilizes applications containing huge amounts of data to facilitate the financial sector with intelligent decision-making capabilities. The advancement in AI by utilizing ML techniques helps the financial industry in detecting hidden patterns and deducing associations. AI's smart recommendation systems facilitate investors and financiers in decisions and long-term plannings. Large volumes of unstructured data can be rapidly standardized by NLP and turned into valuable knowledge. The client experience is another advantage for financial services organizations that are greatly impacted by AI. Beyond simple automation, R-CA can produce corporate results like increased client satisfaction, decreased turnover and higher revenue.

One use of AI in the financial advising sector is automated advisors. It can choose stocks for portfolios depending on the client's desired balance and provide basic financial guidance. Robot advisors, like other expert systems, employ AI technology in conjunction with a knowledge base to approximate the decisions and actions of an experienced human with specialized knowledge in each industry. To enforce greater levels of security, AI-based cyber security systems have been implemented. AI's spam filtering reveals any real-time data and alerts that have been logged for inappropriate content. Malware can be recognized because it can adapt and learn. Companies can utilize data arranging, deletion and storage backups in conjunction with organizational security to protect the deployed applications and platform business activities. GenAI carries out smart statistical analysis to minimize human errors and enhance the banking sector's productivity while also optimizing automated tasks and lowering costs.

Apart from all the advancements, financial institutions will also need to develop robust and unique permission-based digital customer profiles; however, the data they need can be kept in different silos. By removing these obstacles, adding an AI layer and seamlessly integrating human engagement, financial institutions may create solutions that scale while meeting the unique needs of their clients.

Learning Objectives

(1) To understand the importance of AI which provides competitive edge, productivity and technological advancement in the evolution of financial services.
(2) To illustrate the rise of AI in financial services with improved decision-making capabilities.
(3) To identify the recent AI trends, technological development and their adoption in the financial industry.
(4) To analyze and anticipate the future of AI and ML techniques to improve the recent financial advancements more robust.

Chapter 6

The Use of Data in Financial Services

Introduction

Data-driven decision-making is paramount in today's fast-paced and highly competitive environment for the lion's share of financial services. Nevertheless, tech – new tech – in the ever-advancing state of today's environment demands not simply more data but the technology to collect, process, analyze and implement with it. The outcome increasingly demands a complete overhaul, if not a total adjustment, and even a rethinking of the fundamental concepts that support modern financial firms.

If you're hungry, then for a comprehensive exploration of how data are used across the financial sector today, look no further. You've found it in the complete coverage of the financial sector's big data revolution, here.

Within the financial service industry, several data types intertwine, many shaping operations and strategies for diving. From structured financial data (transaction records, market trends, etc.) to unstructured data (like customer feedback, etc.), the doodle-dappery is exhaustive. What's more important than naming these types today is the evolution these elements are undergoing within financial services to define and categorize. Structured data are of a numerical nature and are typically delivered in a predefined format – transactional data, market indices and financial statements for instance. This big data mining can also include unstructured data, such as email, mobile, M2M, social media, video, photos, voice, qualitative market analysis, call centre data and more. Structured data need to be the backbone, so to speak, but when it is complemented by unstructured data you complete the picture.

The Pivotal Role of Data in Shaping Financial Strategies and Decision-Making

The evolution of financial services has been a delightful thing to watch. As data evolved from the role of passive record-keeper to a profound influence of financial strategies and decision-making, those who could skillfully leverage data to optimize strategies, improve operational efficiency and secure competitive advantage

The Global Evolution, Changing Landscape and Future of Financial Markets, 47–57
Copyright © 2025 Syed Ali Raza, Darakhshan Syed, Syed Rizwan and Maiyra Ahmed
Published under exclusive licence by Emerald Publishing Limited
doi:10.1108/978-1-83549-330-420251006

could not only survive but thrive. But the transition from merely 'using data to answer the questions' to using it 'to identify the questions to ask' was perhaps most profoundly impactful of all, marking just one small way that the field was forever changed. No longer would insight and instinct be driving financial institutions (FIs). Rather they had achieved an entirely new state of enlightenment in which data were their guide through the complex new landscape of modern finance.

The hedge fund business is one of the oldest and most data-rich industries on earth – one of the first to realize that what we now call 'big data' could be mined to produce outsized returns. For decades, managers have sifted through the 'alternative' data that populate every sector of our information economy – stock prices, economic indicators, corporate disclosures, future contracts and for the most part, they've used those data just the way you'd think. However, a growing fraction of managers have begun to think creatively about how they could use these data to train machine learning (ML) models. Like the move from fundamental trading algorithms to early sorts of quantitative techniques, not all firms will transition into the sophisticated ML-based tools we've written about in TAP, but the firms that do will have a critical strategic advantage in making sure that data aren't just an input to that are an end in themselves but rather an asset that will help shape their ability to compete down the road (Brewster, 2023).

Data Collection Methods

Traditional Methods vs Modern Approaches

As the industry has shifted from manual, paper-based processes to digital systems, data collection methods have evolved in kind. Manual data entry and periodic reporting are yesterday's news. Today's most forward-thinking FIs collect data in real-time, a strategic shift that streamlines the decision-making process, ensures accuracy and lets finance professionals keep pace with today's ebbs and flows in the marketplace.

Traditional data collection methods involved a significant amount of heavy lifting and were fraught with inaccuracies and mismatches to the industry's hyperspeed. Early iterations of online platforms, APIs and IoT devices introduced automated data collection, providing instant access to the data finance and other lines of business professionals need to immediately react to trends, changes in the market and new regulatory mandates.

The Rise of Big Data and Its Impact on Financial Institutions

The age of big data indeed ushers in a radical leap in data processing capacities within the financial sector. Big data affords FIs a host of attributes such as volume, velocity and variety that critically alter the way that information is managed. Traffic in real time with volumes and varieties of data to large demands advanced tools and technologies for analysis and interpretation. In this instance, big data analytics supports the creation of insights by FIs from large and complex datasets. For example, in no area is this more evident than in relation to risk management, fraud detection and customer relationship management.

Regulatory Considerations in Data Collection

Regulatory considerations are a major consideration as FIs embrace more tactical and effective data collection methods. A variety of rules dictate how sensitive financial information is handled and must be followed in concert with data protection laws, privacy regulations and industry-specific mandates. FIs operating in today's data-centric landscape face a unique challenge, striving for the right balance of compliance and innovation (IIMJ, 2023).

Data Analysis and Interpretation

Tools and Techniques for Analyzing Financial Data

For FIs, swaths of data are valuable only when effectively analyzed. Data analysis tools make it possible for financial professionals to parse through complex datasets and identify unique patterns, thus making more informed decisions. Visualization tools make sure raw data are turned into legible charts and graphs, letting professionals communicate these financial findings to stakeholders. Integrating these is what makes it possible for data to be a strategic asset rather than an overwhelming challenge.

Machine Learning Algorithms and Their Application in Financial Analysis

The arrival of ML algorithms has completely overhauled financial analysis. It has brought with it predictive modelling, pattern recognition and automation. These are capabilities that ML algorithms are particularly good at and their application goes beyond just making sense of financial data. For instance, they can also be used for risk management, fraud detection and algorithmic trading.

In risk management, the self-learning algorithms look for patterns in historical data and make predictions about future trends and potential risks. Analysts protecting against fraud have been using anomaly detection algorithms that spot the unlikely among transactional data where it's being fired across at volumes and speeds until now only dreamt of. Meanwhile, bot traders find their predictive models can make millisecond decisions about their best trades in fast moving markets. There's a cocktail of performance enhancement in financial analysis: by speeding up and driving insights, technology provides institutions using it with a critical edge ('Data Analytics in Banking and Financial Services').[1]

---

[1]IIMJ. (2023). Data Analytics in Banking and Financial Services. Available at: https://www.iimj.ac.in/omdp3-2023

Risk Management Through Data

The Use of Data to Identify and Mitigate Financial Risks

Risk management is critical to financial stability, and leveraging data to effectively identify and mitigate risks is a key piece of the puzzle. FIs leverage historical and real-time data in every way, shape and form to evaluate and manage all their risk types, including credit, market and operational risks.

In credit risk management, for example, real-time transaction data and credit scores can help to determine the likelihood of default. For market risk, you would look at market trends, historical data and any number of geopolitical issues that could cause fluctuations in the market. For operational risk management, meanwhile, a firm could use data to identify errors in processes and systems that would cause a disruption.

Predictive Analytics for Risk Assessment

In an uncertain environment, financial services institutions are increasingly looking for ways to anticipate and proactively manage potential risks, and predictive analytics are showing them the way.

Fuelled by ML algorithms, predictive analytics models give an organization a handle not only on future market trends and customer behaviours but also – especially in the case of predictive risk modelling – potential future risks, improving the ability to make decisions in dynamic and uncertain environments.

What typically happens with these predictive risk models is that, given some historical data, they're 'trained' by ML algorithms to identify patterns and relationships that are critical and on that basis, allow proactive risk mitigation strategies to be put into place and the impact of unforeseen events to be determined.

Real-Time Risk Monitoring in Financial Transactions

The fast-paced world of financial transactions has seen the critical need to have real-time risk monitoring grow all the more important. This need is being met head on by FIs, which are turning to advanced technologies like artificial intelligence (AI), blockchain and real-time analytics to monitor transactions 'as they happen' in real time. This allows 'transactions as they happen' spotting of risks, meaning they can respond to potential risks from a position of knowledge rather than having to be reactionary – fixing after the fact. This is in stark contrast to batch processing methods that would see anomalies, suspicious activities and potential fraud go unnoticed for some time.

The advantage of AI and advanced analytics technologies that provide real-time risk monitoring over traditional approaches is pretty obvious. The old ways couldn't spot weird patterns until they had already started to hurt banks and their customers financially. However, the combination of AI and analytics does more than improve risk management capabilities. It's change that lets the financial ecosystem become both more secure and more resilient (Vaclav, 2023).

Customer Insights and Personalization

Utilizing Data to Understand Customer Behaviour and Preferences

Advances in data analytics capabilities have responded to the demand by enabling financial services providers to analyze customer behaviour and preferences and act upon the insights that emerge. It allows institutions to provide personalized experiences and services that meet customer expectations, and the technology solutions are more affordable and efficient to implement than before.

A 360 view of customer interactions delivers a deep understanding of how customers are interacting, which channels are customers' preferred channels and the frequency of interactions across channels, and the types of products or services that resonate the most with a particular segment within a customer base. Data analytics insights enable institutions to deliver exceptional customer experience (CX), to cultivate lasting customer relationships as well as insight into how CX impacts timely and relevant offers for the individual.

Personalized Financial Services and Products

As the age of one-size-fits-all financial services erodes, data analytics enables FIs to craft bespoke, individualized services attuned to a client's every need and desire. This hyper-personalization affects all aspects of service from the types of marketing campaigns a customer will receive right down to the specifics of a portfolio built just for them.

Ethical Considerations in the Use of Customer Data

When it comes to building personalized financial service offerings, leveraging customer data come with a host of ethical underpinnings. Nimbly tiptoeing the tightrope between using data to help – and respecting customer privacy – becomes a marching order for FIs. Transparency, explicit permission and hardened defenses against any abuses all land top-of-mind in the pantheon of ethical data usage.

Of course, responsible handling of that sensitive customer information is also a must. After all, ensuring that data are used for the intended purposes – and not leveraged to the gain – of financial services firms is critical. Finding the just-right balance between personalization and privacy, after all, isn't just an ethical buy: It's also one that helps foster trust on the part of clients ('The Importance of Data Analytics for Financial Services').[2]

[2]Brewster, K. (2023). The importance of Data Analytics for Financial Services. Available at: https://www.brewsterconsulting.io/the-importance-of-data-analytics-for-financial-services

Fraud Detection and Security

How Data Are Employed in Identifying and Preventing Fraudulent Activities

The stakes are high no matter where you look or what industry you occupy. The proliferation of digital data in the financial services sector has opened doors to new monumental targets for sophisticated cybercriminals.

In the fight to stop them, data are rapidly emerging as financial service's first-line-of-defence. FIs aren't just stopping transactions they should be rejecting through modern systems of questionable popularity and controversy, but they take data on a stroll through algorithms and honeypots engineered to identify and stop them, courtesy of extremely advanced tools.

The conditions under which transactions are made – patterns, anomalies and historical evidence – are the very lifeblood of these systems.

Against this backdrop, these systems utilize AI and ML algorithms in particular to dive into transactional behaviour. They quickly ascertain irregularities that might not be observable at face value and also carry the onerous responsibility of flagging pertinent items for future inspection that run contrary to a financial institution's neatly arrived policies and protocols.

Cybersecurity Measures in Financial Data Management

As FIs shift from a transactions-based to a more data-centric outlook, cybersecurity becomes an ever-graver matter. As institutions proliferate, and the technology that drives them becomes ever-more-integral to the landscape, financial information is more valuable than ever. Cybersecurity is a set of technologies, processes and practices designed to protect networks, computers, programs and data from attack, damage or unauthorized access. It includes encryption, secure authentication using biometrics – like fingerprints or voice recognition – or public/private keys, intrusion detection and a multitude of other techniques.

In the business of keeping data safe, they're just doing it better. Cybersecurity tech in the financial industry is moving forward at a breakneck pace – and for good reason. These days only the most sophisticated of the crooks can catch the data worth the rewards.

Balancing Security With Customer Privacy

But while data security is obviously a top concern, FIs also need to keep in mind the vital importance of consumer privacy. Truly preserving consumer privacy means implementing security measures that protect sensitive data without stepping on the privacy rights of consumers. Building trust means maintaining clear privacy policies that detail consumers' rights to opt out of having their data shared and otherwise choose how their information is shared. So it's incumbent on FIs to be upfront and clear with consumers about what exact use they're making of sensitive data (Igan & Lambert, 2018).

Data Governance and Compliance

Best Practices for Data Governance in Financial Institutions

Effective data governance requires the implementation of best practices, aligning with regulatory requirements and industry standards. FIs deploy comprehensive data governance frameworks incorporating data stewardship, data quality management, and mechanisms for accountability.

Ensuring Compliance With Data Protection Laws

By the nature of things, complying with data protection laws is not a one-time effort but a continuing commitment. Banks and other FIs have implemented sophisticated systems to keep data safe, using everything from encryption to access controls and 'anonymization' of data. These systems were put in place to meet the requirements of various laws that mandate the protection of sensitive data (not to mention to keep that information from falling into the wrong hands).

But these systems get more complicated when data are involved in what data lawyers call 'cross border data flows', i.e. when data travel on the internet to places whose laws are different from those of the main jurisdiction or whose approaches to compliance may be significantly different from those a bank would have known in the past. The question thus becomes: Will the rules be flexible enough to allow the systems used by financial institutions to adapt to the changing data control environment (Corporate Finance Institute, 2023)?

Data Monetization

Exploring Ways in Which Financial Institutions Can Derive Value From Their Data

Data, once seen as a purely operational asset, are now an invaluable resource that holds the potential to generate value. As data become more and more intrinsic to a financial institutions' competitive edge, there are several directions institutions may take to transform data into a strategic asset that can be leveraged to unlock revenue generating opportunities. Strategic partnerships, data marketplaces and novel business models represent three potential paths to explore.

Data as an Asset and Its Potential Revenue Streams

Considered an asset, data are enabling banks to access new streams of revenues including targeted advertising, bespoke market research and tailored product offerings. In some instances, there is scope for banks to licence or sell their datasets to third parties.

The various means by which banks can exploit data as an asset are by no means restricted to external partnerships. Banks are in equal measure able to harness data analytics to generate insights that facilitate operational efficiencies, deliver superior CX and bring new products to market. Recognizing data as an asset is therefore both synonymous with forward-looking innovation and the vital next step on the journey towards a more sustainable and profitable future for banks.

Risks and Ethical Considerations in Data Monetization

FIs need to be cognizant of the ethical considerations and inherent risks associated with data monetization. The desire to tap into the value of data must be balanced against the responsibility to put customers' well-being first. This means that anything that might be used to extract customer insights or value must follow carefully-crafted guidelines for protecting and responsibly using that data. These include transparently communicating with customers about how their data are used, providing explicit consent mechanisms and following strict data protection measures.

But even that may not be enough. The potential for customer data to be misused, accessed by unauthorized parties or have privacy breached means banks must be extremely cautious. From an ethical standpoint, extracting value from data means ensuring its monetization is guided by the bank's or credit union's values and ethics, the expectations of its customers and regulatory requirements.

Challenges and Future Trends

Current Challenges in Managing and Leveraging Financial Data

The journey towards harnessing the full potential of financial data is fraught with challenges. But overcoming these challenges is key to unlocking the transformative power of data. These include

- Data quality and accuracy issues that can provide unreliable insights from fintech findings.
- Interoperability issues that hinder the ability to integrate data from diverse sources and platforms.
- Standardizing data protocols is also key to make sure these sources can communicate seamlessly.
- The lack of skilled talent who can help maximize the value of financial data.

Emerging Technologies and Their Impact on the Future of Data in Financial Services

Their growing influence is set to significantly shape the future of data in financial services. AI, whose algorithms continue to advance and enrich data analytics, will increasingly be consumed to enhance everything from predictive analytics, pattern recognition and classification models to natural language processing, document summarization and robotics and automation.

Blockchain, whose technology will continue to mature, promises to assume a leading role in minimizing fraud through a more secure and transparent system of transaction recordkeeping. Indeed, it enables disparate parties to share access to the same digital ledger of transactions, each with assurance that their copy of the ledger is in sync – without permitting the data visibility and control rights between each other typically associated with the public cloud.

Quantum computing is the biggest wildcard of all. Still nascent, the technology is posed to transform the data capabilities of financial institutions. By manipulating the ability of subatomic particles to exist in more than one state at a time, quantum computers can process significantly more data at greater speeds and promise to solve complex problems that are currently intractable because data on such an astronomical scale is simply beyond the reach of current technology.

Ethical Considerations and the Evolving Landscape of Data Governance

Ethics and technology change in step with one another. The ethical considerations (i.e. regulatory and legal obligations) for financial institutions will revolve around data-driven decision-making, algorithmic transparency and AI (responsible use of). Compliance will further depend on the dynamic, ever morphing landscape of data governance by which ethical standards and practices are upheld. Financial institutions that deploy highly disruptive technologies are compelled to keep pace with ethical consideration as they shift from compliance to regulation and compliance and regulation to the broader impact on society, their customers and all other stakeholders (InterSystem, 2022).

Case Studies and Examples: Wells Fargo & Company's Data-Driven Journey

Real-World Examples of Data Leveraging at Wells Fargo

One look at what the bank does shows it has gone far beyond just using advanced analytics to underpin its operations. Wells Fargo has been at the bleeding edge of applying the big data analytics strategy, and this continued with the creation of a dedicated Tableau powered team – Tableau10 – to aggregate and analyze terabytes of data from the over 70 million customers the California based bank serves globally. The Head of Enterprise Analytics & Data Science at Wells Fargo, Prahalad Thota says:

> The biggest area where big data plays a role is actually organising the data. The data that we collect, it's voluminous, and it's collected from many different sources. (Anoshin et al., 2019)

He added that for this effort, Wells Fargo has been utilizing big data technologies since 2017.

At a high level, taking models from running Python and other programming languages at a subset of the data to the ability to run and apply ML models at scale is the job of the analytics team. In practical terms, Jason Conner, senior vice president for data and analytics at Wells Fargo told TechRepublic:

> That's all theoretical up until a certain point, and what they've been working on is getting us to that certain point. So we recently delivered a product where we can run these models at scale — and by the way, at Wells Fargo, 'scale' is a much different definition than many organizations. (Packin, 2020)

Lessons Learnt From Wells Fargo's Data-Driven Initiatives

Staying relevant in big data environments means Wells Fargo is giving its data analytics team the tools it needs to efficiently wrangle and analyze a diverse data set. Data is more than just information – it's a vital strategic asset that can optimize nearly every aspect of bank operations. The bank's customer segmentation, personalization and risk management efforts are a clear example of why taking a multifaceted approach to data-driven decision making is an effective strategy. Their establishment of a Tableau-powered team shows that investing in skilled data professionals is no longer an option. In a world where data rules, arming a team with expertise in data visualization and analytics means the bank can better translate raw information to actionable insight. As important as investing in tools and technology is, by committing to hiring and retaining talent the bank also underscores the critical role human capital plays in the success of all big data initiatives.

Instances of Challenges Faced and Addressed by Wells Fargo

They've faced some challenges on their data-driven journey to success. Data quality and integration have been significant hurdles for them, particularly when dealing with legacy systems and varied data formats.

In response, Wells Fargo has taken a strategic and tactical approach to migrating and cleansing data in phases while instituting data governance practices ('Big Data in Finance: Benefits, Use Cases, and Examples').[3]

Summary

As we've journeyed along during this deep dive into the role of data in financial services, let's pause to reflect. The insights have been telling, really. Far beyond its utility as the underpinnings of sound financial strategies and solid risk management, data's transformative span has been evidenced in earlier chapters, as it

[3]Corporate Finance Institute (2023).

enhances everything from the broad industry landscape to the most granular elements of the financial services firm's relationship with the customer. Data, it's clear, is the lodestar; the boundless, new frontier of modern finance, fired by a constellation of advanced technologies, ethical considerations, and a decidedly forward-thinking vote.

Learning Objectives

(1) Acknowledge the importance of data as a vital resource for financial decision-making. Examine the development of data usage in financial services historically, noting significant turning points and innovations.
(2) Recognize the different sources from which data is obtained and distinguish between different forms of data that are pertinent to financial services.
(3) Understand big data and how it is changing the way financial institutions make decisions.
(4) Recognize how crucial strong governance and data management systems are to maintaining data security, integrity, and regulatory compliance.
(5) Understand the use of data in financial services to detect, evaluate, and mitigate risks, including real-time monitoring and predictive analytics.
(6) Determine which cutting-edge technology and new trends will influence how the financial sector uses data in the future.
(7) Examine actual instances of financial organizations using data to their advantage, noting the tactics used and the results obtained.
(8) Acknowledge the difficulties and moral dilemmas involved in putting data plans into practice and maintaining them in the financial services industry.

Chapter 7

Blockchain as Enabling Technology

Background of Communication Strategies

After Edward Snowden disclosed highly sensitive data from the National Security Agency in 2013, many people assume that implies that none of your digital assets are protected from being spied on (McCardel, 2022). Yet you can find methods to utilize the internet and irrational mathematics to your advantage to make sure nobody is able to view what you're transmitting to somebody else.

To protect the contents of a message from being discovered by the adversary, the ancient mathematical discipline known as cryptography initially applied to military communications. Authenticating users on a network, verifying the accuracy of sent data and preventing users from repudiating (rejecting ownership of) their transmitted messages are some additional uses for cryptography that have recently been introduced.

Cryptography

Discovering strategies to protect our communications from enemies who may be listening in on us is a significant component of cryptography. It entails identifying systems which can provide us with secrecy. Using techniques to encode information so that attackers cannot read it, encryption is used to achieve much of this.

Yet, encryption is only one aspect of cryptography that goes beyond protecting the privacy of our data. If we go back to our original query, we want to protect the privacy of our conversations and information. Encryption alone is insufficient to do this.

Let's suppose an example: You need to send your pal a very confidential message. So eventually you start learning about encryption and the most recent techniques in order to create your own encrypted channel with your pal. After making sure everything is flawless and checking it again, you send your pal the top-secret message. Regrettably, the person on the other end is not really your buddy (Pachghare, 2019). Unfortunately, your top-secret transmission was intercepted by an adversary, which foiled all of your preparations.

The Global Evolution, Changing Landscape and Future of Financial Markets, 59–79
Copyright © 2025 Syed Ali Raza, Darakhshan Syed, Syed Rizwan and Maiyra Ahmed
Published under exclusive licence by Emerald Publishing Limited
doi:10.1108/978-1-83549-330-420251007

Do you think the aforementioned example is secure? Obviously not. Attacker intercepted your important data in spite of utilizing all the necessary encryption techniques. Your encryption performed a fantastic job of keeping outside parties out of the channel, but it overlooked something crucial: the need to verify that the person on the other side of the channel is indeed who they claim to be. Our communications are kept safe in large part by authentication. If you don't properly verify your communications partner, no amount of encryption will be able to prevent eavesdropping by outside parties (Dechand et al., 2019). Without authentication, you can be transmitting information directly to a foe, as in the case of our example. In cryptography, authentication is carried out via certificate frameworks and tools like digital signatures and public-key encryption.

Integrity and non-repudiation are two more crucial security factors. While non-repudiation prevents the sender from denying that they delivered anything, integrity mechanisms allow receivers to check if information has been altered after it was received.

Cryptography includes all of the mathematical ideas, rules and other processes that can provide us with secrecy, authenticity, integrity and non-repudiation.

We encounter cryptography on a daily basis; however, user could be completely unaware of all that. You might have even utilized cryptography yourself to convey 'secret' messages to your classmates in elementary school, whether you recognize it or not.

How Does Cryptography Work?

Before discussing how cryptography works, let's first talk about the essential terms so that everyone is on the same page.

Plaintext refers to data that's able to read and comprehended with no need for additional security measures. Encryption is the process of masking the contents of plaintext by hiding the appearance of the plaintext. When plaintext is encrypted, the outcome is ciphertext, which is meaningless junk. By using encryption, you may make sure that data are kept secret from anybody for whom it was not meant, including those who are able to see the encrypted data. Decryption is the process of converting ciphertext back to its original plaintext (Aumasson, 2017).

A key seems to be a value which collaborates with a cryptographic method to generate a particular ciphertext. It secures data, much like a real key, so only those who have the relevant key, able to read and use it. The size of key is measured in bits which is directly proportional with the security of ciphertext.

Symmetric Cryptography

Symmetric cryptography, commonly referred to as secret key cryptography, encrypts and decrypts messages using the same key (Agrawal & Mishra, 2012).

Encryption with a symmetric key provides advantages. It proceeds quickly. It works particularly well for securing information that is not being sent (Chandra et al., 2014). Yet, because of the challenges of distributing private keys, using standard encryption alone as a method of transferring secure information can be rather costly.

Sender and recipient must decide on a key and keep it secret between themselves to communicate securely using symmetric-key encryption. If they are separated geographically, they must rely on a messenger, the Bat Phone or another safe method of communication to keep the secret key from being revealed while it is being transmitted. Any information encrypted or authenticated with that key is afterwards readable, modifiable and forgeable by anyone who overhears or intercepts the key in transit.

Asymmetric Cryptography

Asymmetric cryptography offers a solution to key distribution issues. Data are encrypted and decrypted using two distinct but mathematically related cryptographic keys in asymmetric encryption (Rani & Kaur, 2017). A 'Public Key' and a 'Private Key' are the names of these keys. They are together referred to as a 'Public and Private Key Pair'. To everyone, the public key is made available. It is a secret to use the private key. It takes both keys to complete a task. For instance,

- Using the public key to decrypt material that has been encrypted with the private key.
- The private key decrypts data that has been encrypted using the public key.

Digital Signature

The ability to use digital signatures is one of the main advantages of asymmetric cryptography. With the use of a digital signature, the information's recipient may confirm both the integrity and the veracity of the source. Digital signatures using public keys so offer data integrity and authenticity. A digital signature also offers non-repudiation, which prohibits the sender from denying that the information was actually sent (Bromby, 2010). These characteristics are just as essential to cryptography as privacy, if not more so.

How Digital Signature Works

The key pairs used for encryption/decryption and signing/verification are often distinct from one another. The public key is referred to as the verification key, and the private key is referred to as the signature key. Data are sent into the hash function by the signer, which produces the hash. The signature algorithm then generates the digital signature on the supplied hash using the hash value and signature key. The data are given a signature, and both are subsequently submitted to the verifier (Liu et al., 2019).

The verification algorithm is fed by the verifier together with the digital signature and verification key. The outcome of the verification algorithm is something useful. For the data it receives, the verifier likewise uses the same hash algorithm to produce a hash value. This hash value and the results of the verification process are compared for verification.

Hash

Hash is a function that takes the takes the string as an input of any length and generates the string as an output of fixed length.

Hashing is the process of converting a message into an unintelligible string, not to hide the information but rather to confirm its contents (Hadmi et al., 2013). The most frequent application of this is when sending software or huge files, when the publisher makes the program and its hash available for download. A user downloads the program, hashes the downloaded file using the same process and then contrasts the obtained hash with the publisher's hash. If they line up, the download is finished and error-free.

Basic Properties of Hash Function

- It is deterministic (A deterministic function always yields the same result for any given input).
- The computation of hash value is quick.
- The hash value cannot be decrypted (hash value to message).
- A slight modification to a message should result in a significant change in the hash value such that the new hash value looks unrelated to the previous hash value.
- Finding two distinct messages with the same hash value is not possible.

The Rise of Bitcoin

History of Bitcoin

The creation of Bitcoin must be understood in its historical context. The globe was experiencing the worst financial crisis since the Great Depression in 2008. The largest insurer in America, American International Group (AIG), had to be saved by the New York Federal Reserve Bank with an $85 billion loan after the legendary 164-year-old investment bank Lehman Brothers filed for bankruptcy (Burniske & Tatar, 2018).

Several people lost their jobs, while others lost their life savings as the financial system's unrest expanded to other sectors of the economy. This led to rallies and the demonization of individuals in the financial sector who were seen as being responsible for the crisis. Several people started to question if the financial system's design needed to be entirely reevaluated.

Bitcoin

Less than two months after Lehman Brothers filed for bankruptcy, Satoshi Nakamoto published a white paper titled 'Bitcoin: A Peer-to-Peer Electronic Currency System' to the public on 31 October 2008 (Nakamoto & Bitcoin, 2008). Incidentally, the domain 'bitcoin.org' had just been acquired a few weeks before at nonymousspeech.com, a website that enables people to register domain names in an anonymous manner.

Satoshi Nakamoto created a system, which is based on cryptographic evidence rather than trust (Nakamoto, 2009). It enables any two willing parties to deal directly with each other without the requirement for a trusted third party. It was a dramatic change in an architecture. A concept of a peer-to-peer only electronic currency system that would enable internet payments to be transmitted directly from one party to another without going through a banking institution, was given in a white paper.

Bitcoin's Contributions to Innovation

Prior to examining the innovations that Bitcoin introduced, it is crucial to comprehend the issue that it sought to address: our dependency on financial institutions. In the opening sentence of the Bitcoin whitepaper, Satoshi Nakamoto reiterates this point by stating that 'Commerce on the Internet has come to rely almost exclusively on financial institutions serving as trusted third parties to process electronic payments' (Farell, 2015).

Digital assets are prone to this issue. If Sanaullah visits Ali in person and gives him a $5 bill, Ali will check the note to make sure it is genuine and will then take possession of Sanaullah's former $5 bill. That is really peer-to-peer, and Sanaullah couldn't have spent that money elsewhere if he wanted to give it to Ali.

The digital era makes this much more challenging because any kind of digital content can be replicated quickly and simply for free or very little money. For instance, if Sanaullah (and everyone else!) could readily create an infinite number of $5 bills, Ali would not be as eager to believe the $5 money. The double-spend problem is what's happening here.

The double-spend issue, according to Satoshi, has been the fundamental impediment to earlier attempts to establish a digital peer-to-peer payment system. He states in the white paper: We construct an electronic currency as a series of digital signatures. By digitally signing a hash of the preceding transaction and the subsequent owner's public key, each owner transfers ownership of the currency to the following by attaching them to the coin's end. To confirm the chain of ownership, a payee might check the signatures. The issue is that the payee cannot confirm that one of the owners did not spend the coin twice.

The crypto community had long been working to find a solution to the double-spend issue. As an analogy, let's say that whenever I send someone an email, a duplicate of that email is waiting for them in outbox and the receiver's inbox. The identical email would be present in other places if other people were copied on it. While this is incredibly effective for emails, it is ineffective if the email contains any sort of monetary value. The money would be virtually useless if one could 'generate' a limitless supply of it.

In order to solve this problem, we have relied on banks or other reputable central agencies to act as those dependable middlemen or bookkeepers – of course in exchange for a charge. With the use of such middlemen, Sanaullah may only send $5 if he has that amount in his account; if he sends it to Ali, he is no longer in possession of that amount and cannot send it to anyone else.

Nonetheless, the influence of these reliable centralized authority is considerable. Their presence not only raises the system's cost, but it also places more control in the hands of a select few and limits who may use their services for transactions.

Bitcoin's Underlying Technology

According to Auer (2019), cryptography, decentralization, immutability and proof-of-work are four pillars that work together to achieve Bitcoin's objective of doing away with the requirement for a reliable central party.

Bitcoin's Use of Cryptography

Cryptography is the process of securing information through mathematical algorithms or coding. Without cryptography, cryptocurrencies are just a central hub for attackers and scammers. Cryptography helps in encrypting messages and helps them stay confidential to those who need to read them. As it is widely used in various forms of communication, cryptography can be classified according to its method of encryption. Among the most common forms of cryptography include symmetric key encryption and asymmetric key or public key encryption (PKE). Cryptography has become essential in many applications such as e-banking, credit card transactions, financial transactions and digital signatures (Peng, 2013).

A series of digital signatures form the currency is known as Bitcoin. A hash of the previous transaction and the subsequent owner's public key are digitally signed and added to the end of the coin as a means of passing ownership of the currency from one owner to the next. A payee can check the signatures to confirm the ownership chain. Of course, this presents a dilemma since the payee is unable to confirm that one of the owners did not spend the coin twice.

In the traditional world, banks and other reputable central institutions serve as a conventional solution to the double-spend problem. Yet in a society where power is distributed, how can we have this?

Bitcoin's Use of Decentralization

While having a network of bookkeepers might help us solve the double-spend problem, we would also require a 'master bookkeeper' or other gatekeeper. The system becomes more centralized as a result, though.

So, the answer in the Bitcoin network is to let everyone be a bookkeeper and have the same set of books and records as everybody else. Nodes are the name given to these bookkeepers. All transactions are broadcast to the different Bitcoin nodes, allowing anyone and everyone to view them and update their 'books' (Nabilou, 2019).

Yet, how can we be certain of the sequence of these transactions? We need to agree on a certain order of transactions even if everyone can view them all.

This is done by the Bitcoin network through blocks. Each block represents a page if the Bitcoin network were a huge book. The bookkeepers must be aware of what the last page is and how it is formatted so that everyone is 'on the same page'. It would be similar to a large book club where the next page is not turned until everyone in the group has concurred on what the previous page, or in the case of the Bitcoin, what each block, says.

Bitcoin's Use of Immutability

So how are we going to make sure that nobody goes back and edits a page?

Using timestamp servers, the Bitcoin network accomplishes this. A block of items that need to be time stamped is hashed, which then disseminates the hash broadly.[1] The timestamp establishes that data have to be there at the moment in order to be included in the hash, which is clear from the timestamp. In a chain, each timestamp reinforces the timestamps that came before it by include the prior timestamp in its hash.

As we know, the hash of each piece of data will vary even if only a single minor feature is altered. As a result, making the hash of every previous page a part of every page makes it more difficult for someone to update the record because doing so requires changing every page that came before it. The Bitcoin network ensures that when any new piece of information is added to the chain, it becomes immutable since a new block is produced and added to the chain about every 10 minutes.

Bitcoin's Use of Proof of Work

Nevertheless, if everyone is using the same book and we can't continue until we've all agreed on what the last page will say, who will decide what that page will say? We could have a 'master' editor or master bookkeeper, but it would undermine Bitcoin's intended decentralization. Proof of work (PoW) then becomes relevant.

This procedure is known as 'mining.' A hash of the transactions in that block, a hash of the block before it, the time, and a numeric value called the nonce are the four different pieces of information that make up this information (Shi, 2016). The nonce, which is distinct from the transactions listed on that block, is a random integer. Hence, using these four variables, a 'miner' will try to produce a hash that contains the required number of initial zeros. The term 'golden hash'

[1]https://learn.saylor.org/mod/book/view.php?id=36306&chapterid=18885

refers to the result. A nonce of 0 can be used as a starting point, followed by a nonce of 1, a nonce of 2 and so on by the miner. A miner's chances of finding the 'golden hash' – the one that satisfies the criteria and enables him to add that block to the Bitcoin blockchain – increase as he tests more nonces.

The selection of the appropriate hash is thus reduced to a question of sheer coincidence. The next golden hash might potentially be discovered by anyone, in principle. A miner's chances of discovering the ideal hash and earning fresh Bitcoins as a reward increase with the number of possible nonces she may try. At the start, these miners are paid with 12.5 Bitcoin as compensation for their laborious job; however after every 210,000 blocks, this payout is cut in half. The initial transaction of each block is referred to as the 'Coinbase transaction' (Schar & Berentsen, 2020). In addition to paying miners, this payment also serves to mint new Bitcoins.

As per statistics,

New Block creation = 6 per hour → 6*24 → 144 per day
Number of new Bitcoins = 144*12.5 → 1800 per day

But there's a problem here. Then why don't somebody just throw a lot more computers at the problem, increasing the mining hash rate if somehow the key to earning new Bitcoins is to succeed in this chance-based game? Although it would seem attractive, doing so would lead to monetary inflation because it would dramatically reduce the available Bitcoin.

For this reason, Bitcoin uses 'self-regulatory' feature which makes it more difficult to obtain the requisite golden hash by adding zeros to the hash if additional computer power is added to the network. Around every two weeks, this change is made with the goal of having miners locate the golden hash in 10 minutes.

A new block is therefore added to the chain on average every 10 minutes. However, it should be remembered that Satoshi didn't use the term 'blockchain' in his paper.

Theoretically, anyone may sign up for the Bitcoin network, download old blocks, keep track of fresh transactions and look for the elusive golden hash. This openness is a key benefit of the Bitcoin system. However, mining for Bitcoin has become incredibly difficult over time. It is now quite unlikely to simply plug in your laptop and hope to discover the golden hash. The mining industry has seen a rapid evolution of its technology, moving from regular computers' CPUs through graphics cards' GPUs and finally to application-specific integrated circuits (ASICs).

'Evolution of Bitcoin: From Pizza Purchases to Price Volatility and Adoption Growth'

In May 2010, the first-ever Bitcoin transaction for commodities was officially recorded. On May 22 of that year, Laszlo Hanyecz, a fervent proponent of

Bitcoin, provided proof of his successful Bitcoin exchange: he traded 10,000 Bitcoins for two pizzas, which at the time was only about $41. The value of those same 10,000 Bitcoins had increased to millions of dollars by 2017, making it conceivably the most expensive pizza order in history. Consequently, many members of the global cryptocurrency community now observe May 22 as 'Bitcoin Pizza Day'.[2]

The following 10 years saw Bitcoin gradually gain traction. At the end of 2013, its price experienced a significant increase, reaching almost $1,000. However, this optimistic rise was brief, and the price quickly started to fall. Over the next two years, Bitcoin's value continued to decline, reaching a low of about $200. The Bitcoin community faced considerable difficulties during this time due to a number of high-profile occurrences, such as its connection to the arrests related to the Silk Road marketplace and the hacking of the well-known Mt. Gox Bitcoin exchange. Nevertheless, the number of daily confirmed Bitcoin transactions increased over this time, nearly doubling annually, reaching 100,000 by 2015. This indicates that Bitcoin's usage grew throughout this time (Attico, 2020).

Early on, a specialized group of tech-savvy people, including cryptographers, geeks and libertarians, welcomed crypto-assets. But in 2015 and 2016, the environment quickly transformed, drawing students, traders and early investors.

The true game-changer occurred in 2017, when Bitcoin rose from $10,000 to almost $20,000, attracting mainstream media attention from powerhouses like Bloomberg and CNBC and igniting interest in cryptocurrencies all around the world.

Both retail and institutional investors paid substantial attention to crypto-assets in 2017. During Thanksgiving holidays, Coinbase alone established 100,000 new accounts, and exchanges like Binance received a deluge of inquiries (Arslanian, 2022).

However, prices collapsed in 2018, igniting discussions between believers and sceptics. While some, including Christine Lagarde from the IMF, saw possibilities in transforming how people save and invest, Nobel laureate Nouriel Roubini referred to Bitcoin as the 'mother of all scams'.

Expedia and PwC are two large international companies that have started taking Bitcoin, indicating that cryptocurrencies are becoming more and more popular. However, opinions on whether crypto-assets are here to stay or face significant obstacles on their way to becoming widely used vary.

'Bitcoin's Obstacles: Current Issues and Future Prospects'

The history of Bitcoin can be compared to the early years of the internet. Consider Bitcoin to be the first dial-up internet connections. Compared to high-speed broadband today, it was initially quite slow and had limits. Despite the

[2]https://www.coindesk.com/opinion/2024/05/22/happy-bitcoin-pizza-day/#:~:text=On%20May%2022%2C%202010%2C%20Florida,just%20under%20%24700%20million%20today

difficulties at first, the internet developed and became an essential component of contemporary life. Many supporters think that as cryptocurrencies grow more integrated into our financial system, they will significantly evolve and improve, just like the internet did.

Bitcoin faces a number of serious difficulties. First off, although being attractive to traders and speculators, the currency's ongoing price volatility prevents it from serving as a reliable store of value, a quality sought for in assets like blue-chip stocks or gold. Many believe that volatility would decrease as use increases, but this hasn't happened yet, which is preventing broader merchant acceptance.

Second, more legal, regulatory and tax certainty is required. Acceptance by the general public is hindered by uncertainty over tax consequences and legal status. Though such reforms take time, it is encouraging to see how governments, regulators and tax authorities are gradually tackling these issues.

Bitcoin confronts significant technical challenges, notably regarding scalability. Currently, the Visa network processes over 24,000 transactions per second, compared to less than six or seven on the Bitcoin network.[3] This problem hasn't been solved despite numerous attempts, including hard forks (like Bitcoin Cash) and soft forks (like Segregated Witness).

Furthermore, due to its energy-intensive mining process, Bitcoin's ecological impact is a serious issue. The network was anticipated to use roughly 2.55 gigawatts (GW) of power annually as of 2018, which is almost equal to Ireland's average annual use of 3.1 GW (Küfeoglu & Özkuran, 2019). According to recent estimates, the yearly energy consumption of the Bitcoin network, measured in terawatt hours (TWh), may have increased by as much as 400% in the previous year.

Because they are obviously not scalable, the energy requirements of Bitcoin's proof-of-work method raise questions about sustainability. Alternative cryptocurrencies, such proof-of-stake, use less energy-intensive techniques, yet this problem still affects Bitcoin.

The Birth of Blockchain

Surprisingly, the word 'blockchain' isn't used in Satoshi Nakamoto's white paper. The phrase 'blocks are chained' or 'chains of blocks' comes the closest. However, the fundamental idea of generating blocks and joining them in a chain using cryptographic techniques serves as the basis for the Bitcoin network (Judmayer et al., 2022). Because of this, Satoshi is credited with the invention of the blockchain technology.

It is vital to point out that there is no one, singular or unified blockchain technology. Instead, there are numerous independent blockchains, each with its own laws, programming languages, goals and distinctive features.

---

[3]https://crypto.com/university/blockchain-scalability

Consider how the vehicle industry works: there are many different automakers who each produce a variety of models with their unique features and aesthetics. The options include a Ford, Toyota or Tesla, for example. Despite having different personalities, features and user interfaces, they are all used for the same function – transportation.

Think about several game systems like the PlayStation, Xbox and Nintendo Switch. They all provide gaming fun, but each has unique games, user interfaces and features that cater to particular tastes.

In contrast to prior instances where there were just a few competing systems, the blockchain landscape of today includes many distinct networks. While it's likely that a small number of prominent blockchains with sizeable development communities, apps and user bases may emerge in the future, there are many other blockchain networks now existing, each with their own unique properties and objectives.

Properties of Blockchain

Let's define and outline the main features of the majority of blockchains:

Transparency and Decentralization

Decentralized: Blockchains function without a single person in charge or a central authority. Instead, they rely on a distributed network of users (called nodes) who work together to maintain and verify the data contained in the blockchain. Since there is no single point of failure, decentralization improves security and resilience.

Transparent: All network users can see the transactions and data stored on a blockchain. Because of this transparency, anybody may review the full transaction history, enhancing its reliability and lowering the possibility of fraud or manipulation. Since everyone has access to the same ledger, consistency is guaranteed.

Consensus-Driven

Blockchains need a consensus method to determine if transactions are genuine and how they should be added to the ledger. In order to preserve the blockchain's integrity and avoid double-spending, this consensus is necessary. Various blockchain networks utilize various consensus techniques, such as PoW or Proof of Stake (PoS).

Before adding new transactions to the blockchain, network participants must come to an agreement. This agreement guarantees that the ledger is correct and synchronized across all copies.

Immutable

Data that have been stored on the blockchain are very hard to change or remove, if not impossible. Using cryptographic methods like hashing and chaining together blocks, this immutability is made possible.

The blockchain's immutability is a crucial component for preserving its reliability and trustworthiness. By guaranteeing that old records stay the same, it creates a tamper-proof audit trail.

Indeed, while exceptions may exist, decentralization, consensus-driven operation and immutability are prevalent characteristics found in the majority of blockchains. The most significant and fundamental distinction among various blockchains typically centres around whether they fall into the categories of public or private blockchains.

Public blockchains are publicly available networks where anybody can participate, transactions are validated via decentralized consensus procedures and data once recorded are essentially immutable. Ethereum and Bitcoin are a couple of examples.

Private blockchains: In comparison, private blockchains are more constrained and permissioned. Specific entities are permitted access, and consensus processes could be more adaptable. They are often applied in regulated, professional environments.

Challenges in Blockchain Technology Adoption

Regarding blockchain technology, you observed something significant. It comes with its own set of limits and a number of distinctive advantages, but it is not a solution for all problems. Let's examine the drawbacks in more detail.

Anonymity

Anyone may join and conduct transactions on public blockchains like the Bitcoin blockchain without having to divulge their real identity. While the transactions themselves are traceable and recorded on the blockchain, it might be difficult to pinpoint who is responsible for a certain transaction or movement of assets.

Challenges

- Know Your Customer (KYC) and Anti-Money Laundering (AML) Compliance: Many businesses, particularly those subject to regulatory scrutiny, such as financial services, are expected to abide by KYC and AML rules (Moreno et al., 2021). The identification of anyone involved in financial transactions must be confirmed in accordance with these requirements. The public blockchains' pseudonymous nature might make it challenging for enterprises to adhere to these regulations.
- Transaction Monitoring: Some sectors want transaction monitoring in addition to KYC and AML for reasons like fraud prevention and risk assessment. The anonymity of blockchain participants might make it difficult to effectively monitor transactions.

Considerations

Alternative: Private blockchains are being used by various sectors of the economy and organizations to address these issues. Private blockchains adhere to regulatory and compliance standards since participants' identities are known and confirmed. Even though private blockchains give up some of the decentralization and transparency of public blockchains, they provide more control and transparency over member identities.

Info of Good Quality

Even though data on a blockchain cannot be changed, the input determines how accurate the data are. If false or fraudulent information is originally entered, it is permanently incorporated into the blockchain. This underlines how crucial it is to validate data before it is added to the blockchain in order to prevent the 'garbage in, garbage out' issue.

Interoperability

There are no industry standards that are currently universally acknowledged for the infrastructure of blockchain technology. Many blockchains run in silos with little compatibility with other systems. This lack of compatibility may make it difficult for assets and data to move freely between blockchain networks.

Blockchain Adoption

It takes time for blockchain technology to become widely used. Many people and businesses are still only beginning to comprehend and use blockchain technology. It is a huge endeavour, and the switch to blockchain will take some time. People may utilize blockchain-based systems in the future without even being aware of it, similar to how they use the internet now without being aware of the underlying protocols.

Legal Ambiguity

Blockchain technology was not considered while creating the current legal and regulatory frameworks, particularly in highly regulated sectors like banking and healthcare. Compliance with rules controlling data protection, privacy and other legislation is more difficult as a result. Legal principles and standards must be carefully examined and modified to take into account the special features of blockchain technology.

Despite the enormous difficulties previously highlighted, it's critical to emphasize that a worldwide community of people and organizations is actively attempting to overcome these barriers. Major organizations and financial institutions have recently shown growing interest in the blockchain ecosystem, which has been expanding quickly.

Through around 650 equity agreements between 2012 and 2017, blockchain firms raised more than $2.1 billion in traditional venture capital funding. Additionally, approximately 140 equity deals involving blockchain received close to $1.2 billion in investment from significant organizations within the same time period.[4] Additionally, several businesses have taken the initiative to develop internal resources for performing 'proofs of concept'. Decentralized ledger technologies are being tested in controlled settings as part of these proofs of concept to see how they may be used to enhance different elements of their operations.

It's important to recognize that blockchain technology is still in its infancy despite these significant achievements. There is still much to study and learn about this technology's disruptive potential because large organizations have not yet completely utilized it.

Blockchain technology has garnered considerable interest from the financial services sector. Financial firms in this industry have frequently used private or permissioned blockchains for regulated blockchain experiments. The majority of the time, consortiums or cooperative organizations conduct these studies. Financial institutions may test and investigate blockchain technologies through consortiums in a confidential, secure setting.

For instance, famous instances of such consortiums include the Ethereum Enterprise Alliance, Quorum, built by JPMorgan and the Hyperledger Fabric under the Linux Foundation umbrella. Corda was developed by R3. Each of these consortiums has distinct traits and objectives, but they all share the desire to make it possible for financial institutions to test out blockchain technology in ways that are tailored to their particular circumstances.

Use Cases of Blockchain /Applications of Blockchain Technology

Undoubtedly, the old financial system has long relied on complex networks of reliable intermediaries and centralized systems that resemble hub-and-spoke arrangements. However, the development of blockchain technology has opened up a wide range of inventive applications for it. The applications of blockchain go well beyond simply the banking sector. Its distinctive qualities, including as decentralization, transparency and immutability, have sparked innovation in a number of different industries. A few frequent use cases are Regulatory Compliance, Supply Chain Finance, Cross-Border Payments, Trade Finance, Smart Contracts, clearing and settlement and many more.

Blockchain has several applications in the insurance sector, including smart contracts for quick claims processing. For instance, AXA has used the 'fizzy' platform and blockchain smart contracts to automatically pay policyholders for flight delays. These agreements are connected to data on worldwide air traffic, guaranteeing that policyholders are compensated in the event of a delay of two hours or more.

Health insurance processes are being made more transparent and efficient with the use of blockchain technology. Insurance companies can swiftly validate claims

[4]https://nvca.org/wp-content/uploads/2022/03/NVCA-2022-Yearbook-Final.pdf

by securely storing and exchanging medical information on a blockchain, which lowers fraud and administrative expenses. Patients now have more control over their health information, making it possible for them to safely share it with healthcare professionals and insurance. This strategy ensures accurate underwriting while streamlining the claims processing procedure.

Another noteworthy use for blockchain and smart contracts is in land registries, where they make it easier to issue property titles, automate ownership transfers and stop fraudulent transactions. For land purchasers and sellers, this technology has the potential to drastically shorten transaction timelines.

Case Studies

Making Land Registry Revolutionary Using Blockchain Technology[5]

Introduction

Globally, there has been a lengthy history of inefficiency, corruption and a lack of transparency in land register systems. The development of blockchain technology presents a viable answer to these persistent issues. This case study examines how blockchain technology may transform land registration, with a particular emphasis on how it can be used in the fictitious country of 'Digital Land.'

The Challenge

The current land register system at Digital Land is complicated and vulnerable. Records are frequently kept on paper and are prone to theft, fraud and corruption. There is a lack of transparency in the ownership history of properties, and transactions are time- and money-consuming (Vinothiyalakshmi et al., 2022). To guarantee effectiveness, security and reliability, Digital Land plans to update its land register system.

The Blockchain Solution

A land record system powered by blockchain will be used by Digital Land. This is how it goes:

- Tokenization of Land Assets:

Tokenizing land assets is the initial stage. Each parcel of land is represented as a digital asset kept on the blockchain with legal parity. Each land parcel is guaranteed to be unique and immutable by its digital representation.

[5]https://documents1.worldbank.org/curated/en/788081528687836812/text/project-appraisal-document-pad-P159692-SECPO-version-002-0-2-05212018.txt (Accessed: 26 June 2024).

- Ownership Verification:

Current landowners have their ownership converted to blockchain-based digital tokens. This procedure is difficult because it must take into account the subtleties of preexisting land titles, as well as prospective alterations in the future.

- Transparency and Accessibility:

Because the blockchain ledger is open to the public, anybody may examine ownership information, sales and land divisions. The land register system is made more trustworthy and accountable because to this openness.

- Smart Contracts for deals:

Smart contracts are now used in real estate deals. Specific instructions from buyers and sellers are encoded, and when certain conditions are satisfied, they automatically carry out. The exchange procedure is streamlined by this automation.

Challenges and Solutions

- Real World Verification:

The requirement that the register accurately represent the presence and condition of assets in the actual world is a problem for land registries. Legal tools that maintain ownership rights even when parties outside of the blockchain do not accept them as valid are used to remedy this.

- Difficult Transition:

Moving from a system based on paper to one based on blockchain is difficult and requires careful preparation. To guarantee a seamless transition, Digital Land makes investments in strong data transfer and personnel training.

- Flexibility for Future Changes:

The blockchain system is intended to be adaptable, allowing for any future changes or land splits without jeopardizing the integrity of the data.

Results

Significant advantages result from Digital Land switching to a blockchain-based land register system:

- Efficiency:

Property transactions are accelerated, cutting down on both time and expense. Processes are automated by smart contracts, which do away with the need for middlemen.

- Transparency:
- Ownership history is open and verifiable, which reduces fraud and disagreements.
- Security:

The immutability and encryption of the blockchain provide protection against fraud and data manipulation.

- Accessibility:

By guaranteeing public access to land ownership documents, the open ledger promotes system trust.

- Resilience:

The blockchain's distributed architecture ensures continuous availability, even in the event of server outages.

Conclusion

The case study of Digital Land shows how blockchain technology has the potential to transform land register processes. The advantages of increased efficiency, transparency and security make this technological change a tempting proposition for countries looking to modernize their land register systems, despite the hurdles, notably in linking the digital and physical worlds. The development of blockchain-based land registries has considerable promise as additional pilot initiatives and proofs-of-concept become more sophisticated.

Blockchain-Based Supply Chain Traceability Transformation[6]

Introduction

The intricacy of the modern supply chain environment, which crosses international boundaries and involves a wide range of stakeholders, is what distinguishes it. Unfortunately, time-consuming, laborious, ineffective and expensive operations frequently slow down these complex networks. Low traceability and inefficiencies can result in data errors, counterfeit goods and safety issues. Consumers are

[6]https://www.ibm.com/blockchain-supply-chain

simultaneously becoming pickier and demanding greater openness on the provenance and calibre of the things they buy. This case study uses the hypothetical corporation 'SP Supply Corporation' as an example to examine the revolutionary effects of blockchain technology on supply chain traceability.

The Challenge

SP Supply Corporation deals with raw materials, production and distribution across international borders in a disjointed supply chain system (Papanagnou, 2007). For the firm, inefficiencies, a lack of transparency and quality problems have been ongoing obstacles. SP Supply Corporation has to upgrade its supply chain processes in response to the growing consumer need for transparency.

The Blockchain Solution

SP Supply Corporation makes the decision to put in place a blockchain-based solution for supply chain traceability. This is how it goes:

- Transaction Records:

Every transaction in the supply chain is documented on the blockchain, from the purchase of raw materials through the delivery of finished goods. This results in a transparent and unchangeable ledger of all transactions.

- Documents and Verification:

The blockchain is used to produce and maintain all supply chain-related documents, including certificates of origin, quality assurance reports and customs papers. These records may be updated, viewed and verified by the parties concerned, increasing exposure.

- Complete Audit Trail:

The blockchain establishes a thorough audit trail, enabling the tracking of items in real time. This trail not only protects customers against fake goods but also fosters trust in the reliability and calibre of the items, which has a favourable impact on sourcing choices.

- Streamlined Payments:

On the basis of pre-established agreements, financial transactions are started up easily between stakeholders in the supply chain. Delays and financial friction are decreased by this automation.

- IoT Integration:

SP Supply Corporation incorporates smart devices and linked sensors into the whole supply chain. By keeping an eye on the status of containers, these devices make sure that information about temperature, humidity and other crucial factors is recorded on the blockchain. In the event that items are damaged in transportation, this information is essential for final settlements.

Results

Several noteworthy effects result from the use of blockchain technology in SP Supply Corporation's supply chain traceability system:

- Efficiency:

Processing times at every stage of the supply chain are drastically shortened, resulting in lower costs and fewer delays.

- Transparency:

The supply chain is transparent to all stakeholders in real time, fostering confidence.

- Quality Assurance:

SP Supply Corporation can make educated sourcing decisions and ensure the authenticity of its products thanks to an immutable record of product quality.

- Counterfeit Prevention:

By confirming product authenticity, the blockchain's audit trail helps customers avoid buying counterfeit goods.

- Seamless Payments:

Automated financial transactions make payments easier to make and lessen friction in the financial system.

- IoT-Driven Insights:

Connected sensors offer priceless information for preserving product quality and figuring out settlements in the event of harm.

Conclusion

SP Supply Corporation's case study shows how blockchain technology has the potential to completely transform supply chain traceability. Companies may eliminate inefficiencies, improve transparency, guarantee product quality and shield customers from fake goods by using the blockchain. Blockchain technology presents a tempting answer for businesses functioning in intricate, international supply chains as customer demands for transparency continue to rise. The success of SP Supply Corporation is evidence of the disruptive potential of blockchain in the field of supply chain management.

Summary

In this chapter, we set out on a thorough exploration of the world of blockchain technology, beginning with a historical context that highlights the significance of communication techniques and cryptography. We go into the fundamentals of cryptography, exposing the safeguards for digital data and communications. Digital signatures, symmetric and asymmetric cryptography, and hash functions' critical purpose in ensuring data integrity are all included in this.

The focus of the story then shifts to the explosive growth of Bitcoin, a virtual money that has stirred much controversy in the business and technological worlds. We look at its historical foundations, turning points and how it transformed how we view money and value transmission. The chapter examines how Bitcoin has changed financial institutions and set the path for a new era of digital currencies as it further dissects its contributions to innovation.

We examine Bitcoin's complex use of cryptography to safeguard transactions and uphold anonymity by focusing on its technological foundations. We also explore the ideas of immutability and decentralization, clarifying how they are essential to the operation of the Bitcoin network. The PoW consensus method, which protects the blockchain's integrity and the legitimacy of transactions, is examined in this chapter.

The development of Bitcoin is presented in graphic detail, from its humble origins as a way to buy pizza to its current position, which is characterized by price volatility and extensive acceptance. We also discuss the challenges that Bitcoin is now facing and get a sneak peek at its potential future.

It discusses the emergence of blockchain technology as a bigger idea and highlights its salient features, including transparency, decentralization and immutability. The chapter examines the difficulties associated with using blockchain technology, covering anything from concerns about data integrity and anonymity to the complexities of interoperability. It highlights the legal issues surrounding blockchain technology and cryptocurrencies and offers instances of how blockchain is changing many businesses in the real world.

By the end of this chapter, readers should have a thorough knowledge of these important ideas, how they relate to one another and the significant effects they have on the rapidly changing fields of finance and technology. With this information, they are better equipped to navigate the complex world of blockchain technology and all its varied uses.

Learning Objectives

(1) To provide a comprehensive understanding of blockchain technology, including its cryptographic foundations and the crucial role it plays in maintaining safe and open digital communication.
(2) To have a thorough understanding of Bitcoin's development in reshaping the financial environment and the ground-breaking advances it has achieved in both finance and technology.
(3) To recognize potential and problems that result from the implementation of blockchain technology.
(4) To elaborate blockchain technology and its applications is strengthened by the information, enabling them to interact with it successfully.

Chapter 8

The Changing Structure of the Financial Services Industry

Introduction

The financial sector is going through quick and significant changes. Formerly seen as unimportant, fintech firms now play a critical part in fostering innovation, compelling established financial institutions to compete for their business. Furthermore, the possibility of significant technological companies entering the financial industry is growing. This revolution is transforming the whole financial ecosystem and is not merely a struggle between established firms and startups (Bughin et al., 2018). This change will have an impact on how financial products are created, developed, acquired and disseminated in addition to where you may get them.

In this chapter, we look at three closely related elements of how the financial environment is changing:

Platformization of the Customer Experience: We look at how financial services are focusing more on platforms when it comes to providing customer support. Utilizing technology to give customers a smooth and straightforward experience is part of this transition.

Shifting Market Dynamics: We examine how platformization has had a direct impact on how the financial market dynamics have changed. With an emphasis on the function of platforms in facilitating transactions, this covers the buying and selling of financial items.

The Renovation of Back-Office Systems and Infrastructure: In this section, we examine the critical requirement for updating the infrastructure and connected systems that support the whole financial ecosystem. For the building to operate effectively, refurbishment is necessary.

We also explore the governance and societal issues that the financial sector must deal with as it goes through this remarkable shift. These difficulties cover matters of legislation, morality and the overall effect of these developments on society.

The Global Evolution, Changing Landscape and Future of Financial Markets, 81–95
Copyright © 2025 Syed Ali Raza, Darakhshan Syed, Syed Rizwan and Maiyra Ahmed
Published under exclusive licence by Emerald Publishing Limited
doi:10.1108/978-1-83549-330-420251008

Evolution and Disruption in Finance

In the past, growing the network of physical branches was the only surefire way to succeed in banking. Traditional banks were able to draw additional deposits and clients for their range of financial goods because to this growth. Nevertheless, branches weren't just service centres; they also provided excellent chances to develop client relationships, collect vital consumer data and advertise additional items to cement those connections.

By 2023, the banking industry will have undergone a significant transformation as a result of changing consumer preferences, which increasingly favour digital banking channels over conventional physical branches. A crucial research carried out in the United Kingdom from 2017 to 2022 identified this important change. Over those five years, the exhaustive analysis forecast a startling 36% decrease in consumer visits to retail bank locations. The once-common in-person encounters have decreased in this new era, with the typical client visiting a bank office just four times a year. This change is particularly noticeable among younger consumers, especially British millennials, who were predicted to reduce their yearly bank visits to only two by 2022 (Marous, 2017). This change demonstrates the enormous influence of technology on the banking sector, which has compelled conventional financial institutions to innovate and adapt in response to shifting consumer behaviour.

Banks and financial institutions have been driven to reinvent their strategies and offers in this digital-first environment, placing a high priority on the creation of user-friendly digital platforms and attentive customer service.

This change highlights the fundamental shift towards digital banking channels and calls for a thorough reevaluation of how banks interact with their clients and provide their services. For their continued relevance and competitiveness in this changing financial world, traditional banking institutions must adjust to these shifting tastes.

The Digital Revolution in Banking: From In-person to Digital Channels

Customers' decreased reliance on physical branches for their financial requirements has sparked the transition in banking from in-person to digital platforms. The invention of ATMs made it possible to conduct transactions outside of regular banking hours, and other developments like telephone, internet and mobile banking further enhanced convenience by doing away with the need for a physical presence. Financial organizations are looking into exciting new ways to communicate with customers. Smart speakers like the Amazon Echo and Google Home are enabling voice-based interactions, allowing for things like checking your balance. Additionally, the potential for more proactive and frequent client contact is held by the expanding capabilities of mobile devices, which include sensors that may take location, proximity, and weather into account. However, this potential is mostly unexplored by most companies.

Instead of the physical world, the digital one will surely be the main battleground for businesses competing to engage customers in the future years. An ambitious short-term goal established by Toronto-Dominion Bank, a financial institution with its headquarters in North America, is for 90% of all transactions to be completed via self-service options (Arslanian & Fischer, 2019). This tactical change underlines the growing significance of digital channels in satisfying client preferences and wants.

Regrettably for established businesses, this transition towards digital engagement means they are left with a costly infrastructure of physical locations and human resources that no longer generate the same level of value as before. Consequently, many companies have begun the process of streamlining their network of physical branches. As an illustration of this trend, over the years from 2009 to 2015, there was a notable increase in the closure of bank branches, indicating a reduction in the reliance on physical locations for banking services as shown in Fig 1.[1] Meanwhile, the number of new branches opened by existing banks remained relatively low, underscoring the industry's emphasis on digital solutions and the evolving preferences of customers for online and self-service banking options. According to Roy Morgan data, the number of people visiting bank branches in a typical four-week period dropped significantly from 6.50 million in 2014 to 4.73 million in October 2018, representing a substantial decline of 27.2% in just four years.[2] This decline corresponds with the substantial rise in mobile banking usage during the same period (Fig. 2).

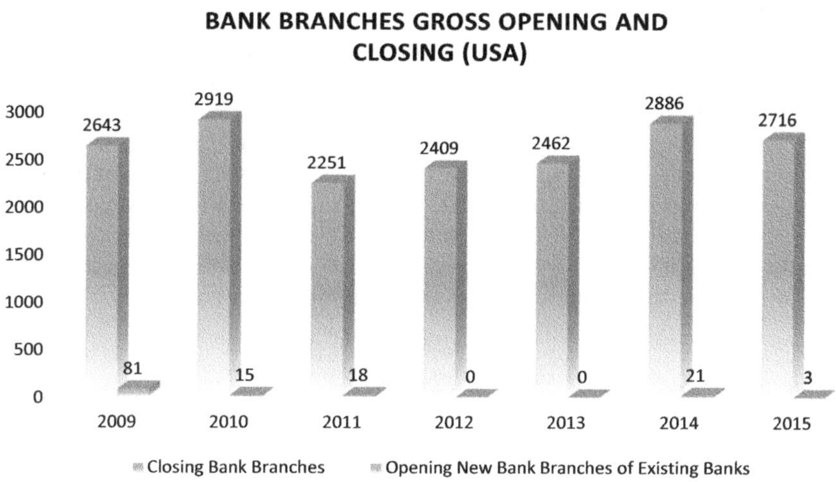

Fig. 1. Declining Trend in Gross New Bank Branch Openings and Closures in the United States.

[1]Wiley: Bankruption Companion Site Content', Wiley, November 2016, https://www.wiley.com/WileyCDA/Section/id-829480.html

[2]'Big Decline in Usage of Bank Branches', Roy Morgan, 30 November 2018, http://www.roymorgan.com/findings/7817-big-decline-in-usage-of-bank-branches-201811300632

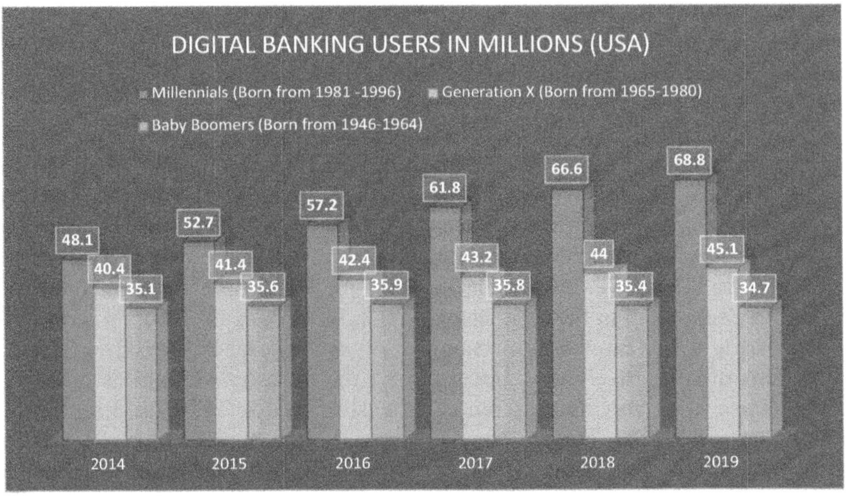

Fig. 2. Increasing Number of Digital Banking Users in the United States (Waupsh, 2016).

For established banks, simply closing down physical branches is not sufficient. Additionally, they must aim to be the best at providing financial services and products through digital channels, a challenge that has proven to be quite difficult. According to a 2018 Capgemini report, only 50% of customers worldwide are satisfied with their banking experiences, which shows there is a lot of potential for improvement.[3] Furthermore, a J.D. Power and Associates survey from the same year showed that in the United States, satisfaction levels among consumers who only use digital banking were noticeably low, underscoring the necessity for banks to improve their digital services and customer experiences.[4]

Gearing up for Substantial Shifts in Finance

Banks, credit unions and other well-established financial institutions make up the conventional structure of the financial services sector, which has mostly remained intact for many years. It may be difficult to imagine the financial ecosystem with a different structure due to its stability. One of the many variables that contributes to the resistance to change is the unexpected loyalty that customers show to their main financial institutions.

[3]IANS, 'Globally, Just Half of Retail Bank Customers Happy with Services: Report', Business Standard India, 21 September 2018, https://www.business-standard.com/article/finance/globally-just-half-ofretail-bank-customers-happy-with-services-report-118092100610_1.html
[4]'2018 U.S. Retail Banking Satisfaction Study', J.D. Power, 26 April 2018, https://www.jdpower.com/business/press-releases/jd-power-2018-us-retail-banking-satisfaction-study.

Customers typically stay with their current institutions for a long time despite frequently expressing unhappiness with their banks and financial service providers. Given the financial industry's quick speed of change and innovation, this commitment is especially impressive and perhaps even illogical. People who have kept their financial relationship with the same institution going for, on average, 17 years are not unusual to discover, for instance, in the United Kingdom.

In order to put this commitment into perspective, it should be noted that the 17-year average tenure with a bank is far longer than the UK's average marital length of 11 years (Collinson, 2013). This direct contrast brings home how long-lasting the bonds between people and their financial institutions are. It calls into question why, in the face of expressed unhappiness, consumers are still so loyal to their banks and highlights the psychological and practical factors that contribute to this commitment.

A number of elements, such as complacency, convenience and a heightened degree of trust that grows with time, may all play a role in the phenomena. Due to the intricacy of financial accounts, direct debits and standing orders, customers sometimes find switching banks to be difficult and may forego looking into other options. This loyalty may also be influenced by the perception of longevity and dependability of institutions as well as the apprehension associated with potential disruption when switching financial partners.

But it's crucial to keep in mind that this picture is rapidly changing, especially with the rise of digital banks and fintech businesses. These new competitors are upending the status quo by providing creative, customer-focused solutions, which may ultimately persuade more people to reevaluate their enduring connections with conventional banks and investigate alternative choices within the financial services ecosystem.

It is difficult to argue that the existing financial ecosystem's structure adequately supports clients' attempts to attain and maintain financial health or reach their financial objectives despite the impressive devotion that many consumers have for their preferred financial institutions. The conventional structure, which is frequently typified by sizeable, product-focused banks, is deficient in numerous crucial areas.

First, despite the fact that most consumers consolidate their financial operations with a single institution, the product-centric structure of these businesses makes it difficult for customers to have a comprehensive picture of their financial situation. It is sometimes difficult for clients to effectively assess their overall financial health because they must juggle a tangle of accounts, each with its own set of terms and conditions. Planning a budget and achieving long-term objectives may be complicated by this splintered perspective.

Furthermore, getting financial counsel is still expensive or contentious. Financial advising services may be provided by traditional banks; however, these services are sometimes accompanied by excessive fees or conflicts of interest because advisers may be compensated to advocate particular products. This may result in advice that is advantageous to the institution but may not be in the client's best interests.

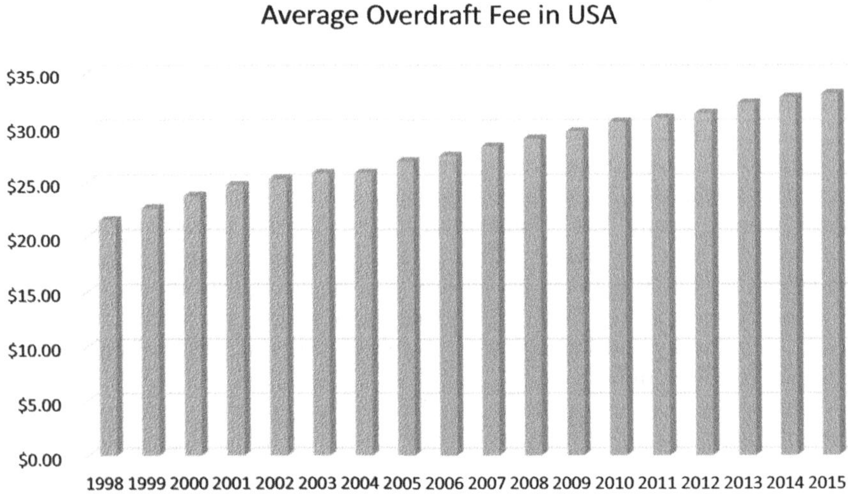

Fig. 3. Average Overdraft Fees in the United States.[5]

Additionally, when customers mismanage their expenditure, the charge structure of banks may ironically benefit the company. Overdraft fees serve as a good illustration of this. Due to clients accidentally overspending their accounts, overdraft costs have been rising over the past 10 years (Fig. 3), and many banks profit from these penalties. This conflict-of-interest results in a scenario where the bank benefits from the mistakes of its customers, which can be bad for their financial well-being and general contentment.

In conclusion, the existing financial ecosystem continues to be characterized by client loyalty, but it is clear that the system falls short in terms of offering a comprehensive assessment of financial health, accessible, unbiased advice and motivating good financial management. In order to achieve more robust financial health and goal accomplishment for all customers, it is necessary to rethink the financial ecosystem with a focus on customer well-being, transparency and fair practices.

The reality for the majority of retail banking customers is very different despite the romanticized image of bankers as 'trusted advisors' to their clients, which is understandable given the ongoing issues within the financial ecosystem. Even while bankers may claim to offer trustworthy counsel, many clients believe that their relationships with their banks are more transactional in nature, focused on everyday financial tasks rather than comprehensive advice and assistance. This discrepancy illustrates the disconnect between the ideal of providing advisory services and the reality for many banking customers, where routine business operations frequently take precedence over individualized guidance and financial empowerment (Fig. 4).

[5]'Average Overdraft Fee | Increase in Average Overdraft Fees, over Time in the United States', Wiley, 2016, https://media.wiley.com/assets/7349/04/web-Accounts-Average_Overdraft_Fee_US.png.

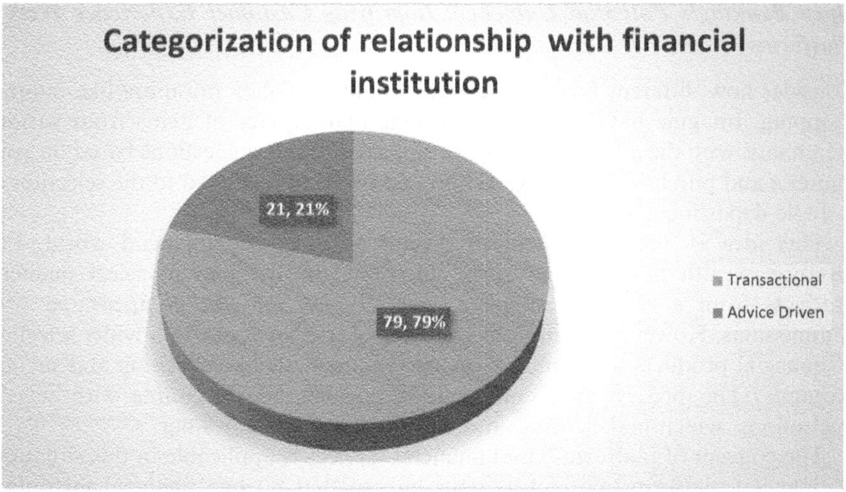

Fig. 4. Banking Relationship in 2015 (US).[6]

Imagine a financial ecosystem where the consumer is at the centre, providing impartial advice and a wide range of bespoke financial solutions powered by AI, crypto and other breakthroughs. The potential of this customer-centred experience will be discussed in the pages that follow.

A Change in Customer Experience Paradigm

Let's compare how people watch television, of course. Many people now use streaming services like Netflix, Amazon Prime or Hulu instead of relying just on one cable provider. These platforms link users to a variety of content producers that offer a selection of programs, films and documentaries. Users gain from a larger variety and on-demand watching, and content providers profit from the platform's user-friendly interface, worldwide audience and tools for content distribution.

Of course, here's another illustration:

Consider the way you look at travel possibilities. You frequently utilize online travel booking services like Expedia, Booking.com or Kayak to book travel rather than being constrained to a particular airline or hotel company. By acting as your connection to numerous airlines, hotels and car rental agencies, these platforms foster competition in the industry. You profit from being able to compare costs, read reviews and access package travel discounts, while suppliers win from the platform's booking and reservation management features and exposure to a larger client base.

[6]'Banking Relationship in 2015 (U.S.)', Wiley, 2016, https://media.wiley.com/assets/7350/52/web-Trust-Banking_Relationship_In_2015_US.png.

Open Banking's Potential Unlocked: Improving Customer Experience With Platforms

Consider how different financial services would be if they ran more like internet shopping. Imagine having access to a huge marketplace of items from various merchants, with the added benefit of getting specialized suggestions based on your interests and purchasing history, as opposed to being restricted to the selection of a single department store.

This idea is already present in several areas of the financial world. For instance, wealth management gives customers the freedom to select financial products from a range of suppliers, yet advisers may be compensated with commissions. However, it might be challenging to gain access to a wider selection of financial products for regular banking requirements like checking and savings accounts. The process frequently entails opening new accounts with several institutions, which makes things more difficult for the consumer.

The concept of platform-based financial services is applicable in this situation. A financial platform may act as your hub so that no one financial institution controls your whole banking experience. It links you up with a wide range of financial solutions from multiple suppliers and makes tailored suggestions based on your financial information and individual needs.

Given that they already control a large portion of the financial process, ranging from consumer contacts to the primary financial assets, such as deposits required to construct financial products, you might be perplexed as to why established banks and financial organizations would support such a system. Why would they give up this much power?

The answer may lay in the evolving regulatory environment, notably the idea of 'open banking'. The creation of safe channels enabling consumers to communicate their financial information with third parties and, in certain situations, to provide those third parties the power to handle client funds, are requirements of open banking rules. Despite the fact that the specifics of these laws differ by location, they are now being actively examined or put into effect in a number of places throughout the world, including the European Union, the United Kingdom, Canada, Japan, and Australia. The Dodd-Frank Act of 2010 urged that open banking be implemented in the United States. Although the time and scope of implementation are yet unknown, open banking has the potential to threaten conventional banking models by reducing the institutions' control over (Treasury, 2018).

Although open banking does not mandate that banks make their goods available on third-party platforms, it does put their control over the client relationship in jeopardy. It makes it simpler for users to utilize a bank's products without directly interacting with the bank, paving the way for new platforms that provide customers access to financial goods from third parties without having to give up their current products. These systems may merge data on a customer's existing financial products with any new ones they acquire by utilizing open data.

Future Financial Platform Owners: Who Will They Be?

A crucial question arises in the drive to build a revolutionary financial services platform: who has the skills necessary to undertake such a groundbreaking project? It takes a special combination of abilities and resources to complete this enormous project. The platform must be skilled at creating cutting-edge, customer-focused digital experiences and at bringing together a varied range of partners that each provide financial goods in an effortless manner. Additionally, it must be able to offer automated financial advice and product suggestions to users that are useful. In terms of regulation, it must be knowledgeable about the complex guidelines that control the distribution of financial goods. Notably, unless it decides to consciously offer those services directly, the platform need not necessarily manage the more complicated rules regulating fundamental banking activities like keeping deposits or producing financial products.

Today's tech behemoths like Amazon, Apple, Google and Facebook suit this description extremely well. They have the resources, client base and data analytics skills needed to develop into platforms for the delivery of financial services. Instead of assuming the role of full-fledged banks, they may concentrate on providing access to a wide range of financial products for users while tailoring suggestions based on user information and preferences. These internet titans can drastically alter the financial environment without copying conventional banking institutions by using their already large user bases and technologically advanced infrastructure.

Parallel to that, this paradigm change is similar to how Chinese digital behemoths Alibaba and Tencent have operated. They have established vast ecosystems that provide customers with a wide range of financial goods and services, dominating the Chinese consumer financial services sector. This shows how a cutting-edge platform approach may offer a one-stop shop for consumers' financial requirements, from payments to investing. At the same time, neobanks like Revolut, Monzo and N26 have the chance to take use of open banking legislation to improve client insights and work with diverse financial product suppliers.

Some reputable financial institutions are entering the platform market in response. The Dutch bank ING, for instance, places a strong emphasis on the value of open digital platforms for providing consumers with a variety of options, even if not all of these options are in-house (Arslanian et al., 2019). However, legacy systems and data fragmentation are problems that conventional financial organizations must deal with. Although they have the confidence of their clients and a thorough grasp of financial laws, they must quickly adapt to new technology and restructure their operating models in order to survive in the changing financial environment. For incumbents, the transition to becoming financial platforms marks a turning point that necessitates innovation and agility to survive in the digital era.

A Platform Model of Customer Experience Faces Wider Challenges

No matter who runs these platforms, if financial platforms become the standard method for providing financial goods and services to consumers and small-business owners, a number of important challenges need to be resolved.

First, we may learn from platform models used in other sectors of the economy where network effects are important. A platform's worth rises as it expands and draws more users, producing a cycle that reinforces itself (Shelanski et al., 2017). This means that, in contrast to traditional corporate structures, industries where platforms are dominant often have fewer rival companies. The growth of platforms in the financial sector may result in fewer institutions actively managing client connections. Similar to what has happened in Europe with digital media and retail platforms like Google and Amazon, this may catch the eye of antitrust regulators.

For instance, there can be worries about market concentration and possibly anti-competitive activity if a small number of financial platforms dominate the industry. Similar circumstances have occurred in the internet sector, where massive companies like Facebook and Google have come under fire for their data practices and market dominance. Regulators may need to make sure that there is still a reasonable amount of competition and that customers' options are not overly constrained.

Second, the need for safeguarding consumer data grows as the financial sector shifts towards platform distribution. Although the platform approach can improve access to guidance, product suggestions and customisation, it mainly depends on exploiting consumers' financial and non-financial data. This raises concerns regarding consent, security and data privacy. Customers must be able to decide how their data are shared, understand how they are used and guarantee its security. To do this, digital identification systems must be improved so that users may safely control their data.[7]

Take the General Data Protection Regulation (GDPR) of the European Union as an illustration of the necessity for stringent data protection procedures. The GDPR provides individuals more control over their personal data, including the ability to access, be informed about and request the deletion of their data. Similar laws could be required to protect clients' financial information when they interact with financial platforms.

Last but not least, these platforms' business structures must be transparent. Customers need to be fully informed of a platform's business model, including any commissions, subscription costs, advertising fees and data sales to third parties. Customers need this openness in order to understand how the revenue model of the platform may affect the items they see and the suggestions they get. Addressing any conflicts of interest is also essential. Customers should be aware, for instance, if a platform recommends certain items because they are actually suitable or because doing so would result in larger commissions if the platform earns commissions for products sold.

Think about social media sites and their advertising structures for a real-world illustration. Users are getting more and more worried about how advertisements

---

[7]Rohan Pinto, 'The Role Of Verified Digital Identities In The Open Banking Ecosystem', Forbes, 11 December 2018, https://www.forbes.com/sites/forbestechcouncil/2018/12/11/the-role-of-verifieddigital-identities-in-the-open-banking-ecosystem/

and sponsored content may affect their experiences. Platforms like Facebook have responded by making efforts to increase ad transparency and give users greater control over their ad selections.

For a real-world example, consider social media platforms and their advertising models. Users are increasingly concerned about the impact of ads and promoted content on their experiences. In response, platforms like Facebook have taken steps to provide more transparency regarding ads and allow users to control their ad preferences.

In conclusion, the shift to financial platforms is a gradual one that is influenced by changing consumer preferences and technical improvements. But as the digital world develops, change is happening more quickly. To maintain strong customer trust and adapt consumer safeguards to this changing world of financial customer experiences, both the public and private sectors must collaborate.

Competing in the Developing Financial Product Market: A Changing Environment

There are substantial shifts for individuals who design and sell financial goods as financial experiences and product distribution move to digital platforms. In the past, consumers were mostly captive to the offerings of financial institutions, but in the current environment, customers have the ability to evaluate goods from different financial institutions quickly. Success no longer depends on having a product that is only 'pretty competitive'. Offering the greatest pricing or delivering a specifically tailored fit to individual or organizational demands are the two main paths to success when clients experience little friction when utilizing items from various organizations.

With this change, the financial market is probably going to adopt a 'superstars and long tails' structure. It implies that 'winners-take-all' dynamics will be in play together with an increase in the diversity of niche products, resulting in a market with a few dominating businesses and a lot of quick-thinking specialized competitors. Numerous fast digitizing industries, including music and retail, have seen this tendency.[8]

Think about the dynamics of volume in this situation. By utilizing their size, they may offer very standardized financial products with incredibly little profit margins. The current exchange-traded fund (ETF) market is a great illustration. An ETF's fixed operational costs can be split among a broader client base as its assets under management increase, lowering the cost per unit. Large-scale companies like BlackRock and Vanguard are able to do this because it allows them to charge extremely low fees for their funds, which attracts a larger part of the ETF market and creates a positive feedback cycle that enables them to charge even

---

[8]Erik Brynjolfsson, Hu (Jeffrey) Yu, and Michael D. Smith, 'Long Tails Versus Superstars: The Effect of IT on Product Variety and Sales Concentration Patterns' (MIT Center for Digital Business, September, 2010), http://ebusiness.mit.edu/erik/Long%20Tails%20Versus%20Superstars.pdf

lower costs. The three biggest providers currently control more than 70% of all ETF assets worldwide.[9]

Product makers that cannot or do not want to compete on price are on the opposite side of this dynamic. They'll need to figure out how to compete based on how distinctive their offers are. This might entail adding new features, offering non-monetary advantages or developing highly personalized goods catered to certain client subgroups. Access to client data, most likely gathered via the platform, becomes a crucial resource for these businesses to facilitate personalization. Similar to how online shops enhance their Amazon and Google rankings, these specialized businesses must likewise understand the nuances of the platform's recommendation algorithms.

Players with existing scale who can leverage that scale to develop dominance in particular product categories benefit from the 'superstars and long tails' dynamics. At the same time, it rewards nimble businesses, especially fintechs, that can quickly implement and refine new product offers. The platform ecosystem's bigger, more cost-effective firms and the agile, specialized entrants may squeeze out mid-sized banks, which have historically excelled in a wide range of product categories. To stay competitive, they must adjust to this changing environment, either by gaining size or by identifying a special niche in which they may succeed.

The development of the retail sector provides a practical illustration. E-commerce behemoths like Amazon have put established brick-and-mortar businesses under intense pressure by using their size to provide competitive price and consumer convenience. Smaller, more specialist e-commerce companies, on the other hand, prosper by providing distinctive, niche goods and experiences catered to certain client interests.

Reviving the Foundation: Modernizing Shared Financial Infrastructure and Back Office

The planned reforms to the financial ecosystem would significantly improve user experiences and competitiveness, but in order for the financial system to fully serve clients, it is crucial to update infrastructure and compliance processes.

Streamlining Compliance Functions

It's common to describe the technology infrastructure supporting current financial institutions as a confusing, out-of-date muddle. These legacy systems, which are typically decades old and have undergone a maze of patches, upgrades and one-off integrations throughout the years, are discussed throughout this book. As a result, organizations must use expensive, rigid technology that enforces an outdated, product-centric structure and limits organizational adaptability. As the

[9]Trefis Team, 'Five Largest ETF Providers Manage Almost 90% Of The $3 Trillion U.S. ETF Industry', Forbes, 24 August 2017, https://www.forbes.com/sites/greatspeculations/2017/08/24/five-largest-etfproviders-manage-almost-90-of-the-3-trillion-u-s-etf-industry/

financial landscape changes, these restrictions limit the strategic alternatives accessible to incumbents. These organizations must migrate away from outdated systems if they want to become high-scale 'superstars', agile specialized product manufacturers or customer-centric platforms.

Large financial institutions are increasingly relying on cloud technology as a way to get rid of the limitations imposed by their legacy systems. The transformation has the potential to increase efficiency and scalability, giving firms the flexibility to change how they use their resources. Additionally, by being re-engineered for the cloud, existing apps may promote better agility, allowing incumbents to develop and roll out new product interactions more quickly (Citi, 2018).

Take the shift of a conventional bank to cloud-based operations as an illustration. They may process transactions more quickly and scale up resources at busy periods, like as the end of the month, by moving their core banking operations to the cloud. Due to smoother and quicker transactions, this not only increases operational effectiveness but also improves the client experience.

Through standardized and secure application program interfaces (APIs), incumbents that transition to cloud-based systems also minimize integration barriers with external service providers. This makes it easier to integrate specialist service providers, such as regtechs, into the operations of an established financial institution. These suppliers can give sophisticated compliance and risk assessment solutions that the incumbent may be unable to supply in the context of regtech. Financial institutions are able to outsource particular back-office tasks as a consequence, allowing them to concentrate on their core competencies. To focus on its core banking services, a bank may, for example, outsource the customer onboarding procedures to a specialist regtech vendor.

This move towards specialized outsourcing may cause conventional 'jack-of-all-trades' banks to become more focused and agile actors in the changing financial landscape. Only the back-office tasks that provide these institutions a competitive edge may be retained, while other specialized tasks may be outsourced to outside suppliers. This improves the overall efficiency and innovation capacities of the financial ecosystem while streamlining processes and enabling incumbents to access specialist knowledge and resources.

Challenges and Opportunities in Financial Infrastructure Upgrade

A serious issue is the Western world's essential financial infrastructure's deteriorating condition. The contemporary economy depends on components like national clearing houses for domestic payments, international payment systems like SWIFT and securities clearing houses. Despite the possibility of real-time transactions, they rely on antiquated technology and business procedures that frequently cause lengthy processing times. Additionally, the vulnerability of these infrastructure parts to cyber assaults is growing. Financial crises might be sparked by instances of bad actors breaking into networks like SWIFT and diverting substantial quantities of money, which not only erodes confidence in financial institutions (Borghard, 2018).

Think of a national clearing house that handles domestic payments as an example. Payments between banks may take longer to complete due to antiquated procedures and obsolete technology. This latency might impede economic activity in a real-time economy when companies and consumers anticipate rapid transactions. Furthermore, system flaws might seriously affect the economy by upsetting the whole financial ecosystem, whether as a result of outdated infrastructure or cyberattacks.

Along with these strong arguments in favour of infrastructure replacement, it's critical to understand the advantages of incorporating cutting-edge technology into these systems. For instance, artificial intelligence (AI) tools have the potential to greatly improve the real-time identification of fraudulent operations, financial crimes and unlawful behaviours. Let's say a payment clearing house uses AI-based fraud detection tools. That way, it may create a more secure and effective financial ecosystem by proactively identifying suspicious transactions and preventing possible losses.

However, modernizing financial infrastructure has challenges that go beyond technology. The new infrastructure must amass a sufficient number of users who agree to accept it and adhere to its usage guidelines, regardless of whether it is constructed in the cloud, based on blockchain technology, or driven by AI. A significant difficulty in advancing the development of financial infrastructure in the years to come will be achieving the required coordination and alignment of vision across various financial institutions, regulators and industry players. In order to maintain the seamless and secure functioning of contemporary financial systems, cooperation, standardization and regulatory assistance will play essential roles in this process.

Summary

This chapter examines how the financial services sector's structure is changing, highlighting the sector's continual evolution and upheaval. The discussion of the digital revolution in banking begins with an emphasis on the shift from analog to digital channels, where client connection is increasingly occurring in the digital realm.

Through the perspective of open banking has the ability to improve customers' interactions with financial systems, it focuses on the paradigm change in the customer experience. Additionally, it raises concerns about the potential difficulties in delivering a platform-based customer experience and the identity of the owners of future financial platforms.

It also explores the evolving dynamics of competition in the expanding financial product sector. The change towards a 'superstars and long tails' market structure, where a select few big firms and numerous specialized players predominate, poses difficulties for mid-sized banks and is discussed in the article.

In the last, it concludes by highlighting the importance of updating shared financial infrastructure and back-office functions. It covers optimizing compliance procedures as well as the difficulties and benefits of modernizing financial infrastructure to suit the needs of a real-time, digital financial ecosystem.

Learning Objectives

(1) To give a thorough grasp of how the financial services sector is currently changing and being disrupted.
(2) To investigate the banking industry's digital transformation, following its shift from conventional in-person services to a largely digital environment.
(3) To study the evolving paradigms in customer experience.
(4) To recognize the important players who will likely control and run future financial platforms and examine the opportunities and constraints presented by participating in the developing financial product industry.
(5) To understand the complexity to modernize common financial infrastructure and back-office procedures, especially in the context of compliance activities, to remain competitive in this sector that is changing so quickly.

Chapter 9

Regulatory, Governance and Future Trends in the Financial System

Introduction

As we dive into the concluding portion of this thorough investigation, it is important to recognize the momentous path that the financial industry has undertaken. This journey, painstakingly traced from the earliest notions of currency to its present state as a multifaceted, technologically advanced system, began with humble forms of monetary exchange, developed through the introduction of coined currency, the intricate economies of past societies and the intricate web of contemporary financial establishments. The narrative has evolved, delving into the digital age propelled by the rise of the internet, the crucial impact of data, artificial intelligence (AI) and blockchain and the significant transformations in the sector's organizational framework (Aldoseri et al., 2024).

In an ever-developing environment, the existence of a strong legal framework and an effective governance structure assumes unparalleled importance. Complex and interconnected economic activities increase the risk potential and policy implications, thus requiring a more sophisticated approach to regulation and governance (Van Asselt & Renn, 2011). These policies are not only protective barriers, but they are key to driving innovation, ensuring stability and maintaining consumer confidence in this dynamic ecosystem.

To put together the basis for this concluding discussion is to understand the complex interplay of governance, law and rising trends within the economy This chapter seeks to demystify those complexities with the aid of dropping mild on how governance examples are regulators who make changes or are approximately to make modifications and could cope with the statistical views presented, as well as contemporary challenges and challenges. Preparing the floor for this concluding discussion includes information on the problematic interplay among governance, regulation and emerging traits inside the financial zone.

This bankruptcy seeks to demystify this complexity via losing mind on the ways governance fashions and regulatory government are adapting, or need to adapt, to the relentless tempo of technological improvements and market

The Global Evolution, Changing Landscape and Future of Financial Markets, 97–118
Copyright © 2025 Syed Ali Raza, Darakhshan Syed, Syed Rizwan and Maiyra Ahmed
Published under exclusive licence by Emerald Publishing Limited
doi:10.1108/978-1-83549-330-420251009

adjustments. Focus will be placed at the strategies and foresight vital for charting the uncharted waters of the destiny, at the same time as also addressing the demanding situations and intricacies of the existing.

The Financial System's Shape and the Value of Regulation

Financial regulations are the laws and policies that control financial institutions. Priorities for financial institution laws include protecting consumer interests, fostering fair competition, maintaining the soundness of the financial system, preventing and minimizing illegal financial transactions. By the mid-1970s, developments driven by the market had abolished a series of corporate restrictions on the ability of financial institutions to make investments, lowered interest rate rules and managed the movement of money across international borders.[1] These developments had led to a liberalization of the global financial system. Financial sector regulation is currently trending towards increased cross-sector integration of financial supervising.

An Historic View on the Effects of Financial Market Regulations

The inception of financial establishments predates the arrival of financial guidelines. Initially, rules were rudimentary, typically geared towards keeping forex stability and preventing fraud. Instead of this, the financial markets continuous to get more complex with time that ultimately necessitates dependence towards an absolute regulatory framework. The main goals of financial organization regulation are consumer protection, unbiased competition and macroeconomic stability in the system (Davies & Green, 2013). The normal operation of financial markets can be disrupted by the collapse of a financial institution, demonstrating how stability is crucial. An equal opportunity for market entry is a prerequisite for a fair competitive environment. A power imbalance results from the knowledge asymmetry that exists between customers and businesses. Customers might not have the necessary knowledge in this situation to choose financial goods and services with confidence. Financial crises typically provide a significant push for new rules and stronger oversight.

Due to the expansion of global corporations and the international character of financial markets, regulations are now essential in today's financial circumstances. Global economic downturns typically have disastrous effects. Risk regulatory regimes now include anticipating risks and planning for their control as essential components. Liquidity drained up during the 2007 financial crisis because financial institutions were unable to identify certain shocks that cause contagion and other externalities (Gaiet al., 2011). In actuality, the crisis had been caused by organizations' excessive risk-taking. It was hard for big organizations to identify risks. As a matter of fact, when American International Group (AIG) failed, 95%

---

[1]https://nap.nationalacademies.org/read/2134/chapter/3

of its business units were profitable. Despite having 125,000 workers, 80 of them were the ones that caused the company to collapse (Prager, 2013).

In addition to protecting investors and promoting macroeconomic stability, effective financial regulation can also minimize the negative impacts of financial failures on the whole economy. Enhancing market transparency can also be accomplished through financial regulation. However, the economy and regulated businesses must bear several expenses because of financial regulation. These expenses include expenses related to the administration and execution of regulations, compliance-related costs and financial market distorting costs. Many of these costs are eventually transferred to the actual economy, hurting the earnings of regulated enterprises. Even after the 2007–2009 financial crisis, the United States' financial regulatory frameworks are frequently regarded as some of the most advanced, extensive, successful and widely imitated in the world (Dam, 2009). However, there are still many issues with these systems, and a lot of research has been done to better understand how financial regulation works. In response to changes in regulations (and tax rates), businesses frequently look for more desirable locations to conduct business. According to Macey (2003), regulatory globalization is a strategy that regulatory bodies might use to increase their influence.

Regulatory Standards and Their Implications on Sustainable and Financial Advancement

There is no doubt about the state's vital role in regulating and overseeing financial systems. State governments around the world oversee a variety of tasks, including bolstering the financial system, maintaining equitable competition and enforcing strict macroeconomic oversight. Fostering financial stability requires robust organizational structures. The financial sector can operate more efficiently with good regulatory policies (Stein, 2012).

Other banks may experience a knock-on effect from the demise of one bank. Stressful situations arise when other banks' creditors and depositors get frightened and anxious. This phenomenon of behaviour is known as 'contagion,' whereby a bank's failure can put other strong financial institutions under strain, ultimately leading to a financial crisis (Gorton, 2015). This is an example of a bank raid. To prevent possible externalities, the state can regulate and supervise big financial organizations to reduce their level of risk-taking.

Government-owned financial institutions increased their lending to the private sector when private banks reduced their funding due to the crisis. Many nations depended on credit guarantee schemes. Several non-traditional fiscal and monetary policies were employed by other nations to support their credit markets. State-owned banks in Brazil were permitted to purchase loan portfolios from financial institutions experiencing liquidity issues as well as equity stakes from private banks. To encourage expansion, state-owned banks in China extended financing to industries. Large corporations in Mexico were given credit by the government-owned development financial institutions. State-owned financial institutions in Germany expanded their lending to large corporations experiencing transient cash flow issues. To increase lending to small- and medium-sized businesses, the Finnish government increased the ceiling on export and domestic funding for the nation's state-owned bank (Barros, 2008).

States were crucial in averting even worse outcomes during the crisis by providing substantial rescue packages and monetary measures. The Financial Stability Board (FSB) was tasked by the G-20 with promoting the coordinated creation and application of efficient financial sector, supervisory and regulatory policies on a worldwide scale (Viola, 2013). Within the structure of Basel III, the Basel Committee on Banking Supervision (BCBS) developed new capital and liquidity criteria for banks.

The Current Legal Structures Supervising Financial Digital Shifts

The rapid pace of the revolution in the finance industry has compelled regulatory bodies to adjust and evolve. These measures aim to address risks related to stability, transparency and customer protection while embracing the advantages of innovation. Below is the detail of the frameworks governing the digital transition, within the finance sector:

Financial institutions involved in dealing with cryptocurrencies must adhere to Anti Money Laundering (AML). Know Your Customer (KYC) regulations to discourage illicit transactions. This involves examining transaction patterns, flagging and reporting activities and verifying the identities of customers. Some governments are implementing sandboxes that allow DeFi startups to test and refine their services in a flexible environment (Allen, 2019). This approach aims to strike a balance between innovation, consumer protection and system stability. The importance of contracts in DeFi has attracted attention towards ensuring their security and compliance with established requirements. As a result, audits and compliance tests are becoming common practices.

According to the regulatory system, the security regulations make cryptocurrencies and digital assets as means of secure transactions. As they followed the complete procedure of registration, accountability of disclosure and confirmation of satisfying the established standards (Girasa, 2018). By classifying cryptocurrencies as assets, commodities or currencies in accordance with legal frameworks, tax authorities throughout states have developed criteria for taxing the digital currency.

With blockchain's integration into economic offerings, adherence to data safety legal guidelines just like the GDPR in the EU is paramount. Safeguarding the confidentiality and protection of private information stored on blockchains is a primary regulatory subject. As monetary entities embody blockchain, the want for standards selling interoperability and seamless integration with current economic infrastructures is emphasized by using regulators to control systemic dangers successfully.

Specific e-cash regulations have been hooked up in diverse international locations, specializing in licencing, capital adequacy and operational recommendations to hold the stability and reliability of virtual price structures. Regions just like the EU have implemented directives which includes PSD2, fostering innovation and opposition in virtual bills whilst making sure stringent consumer protection and safety features (Eriksen & Alne, 2019).

Regulators are increasingly adopting RegTech answers to automate and beautify the performance of data reporting, compliance tracking and regulatory oversight. A collaborative approach is emerging among regulatory government, monetary establishments and generation corporations to create shared standards and frameworks that guide the adoption of RegTech ideas for solving the faced challenges.

The Four Principles

The increasing attention that intellectual and the development of policies communities are giving to the organizational and governance elements of financial sector regulators reflects the realization that financial regulators play a significant role in the contemporary, corporate compliance-driven financial markets. It would be accurate to say, after decades of lack of attention, that financial regulators are 'emancipating' an organization (Mehrpouya & Djelic, 2014). Over the last 20 years, many nations have reorganized their oversight organizations and begun to focus on governance aspects. The organization of supervision and supervisory governance has received a lot of attention recently, mostly in reference to changes in the financial sector. On the contrary, this focus also needs to be seen in the context of a broader emphasis on the establishment of regulatory bodies in several economic industries. In fact, the idea of a regulatory body operating independently of the government is relatively novel for most nations. Most nations now acknowledge that independent organizations with distinct objectives are now an essential part of good governance in their liberalized economy. The acceptance of these organizations does not, however, mean that governments are not having difficulty integrating these new organizations into existing legislative and administrative frameworks. One of the most significant problems here is to give them the proper governance elements.

Independence, transparency, accountability and integrity are the four fundamental principles of good regulatory governance, according to Das and Quintyn (2002). These four guiding principles can support the most important components of regulatory organizations' internal and external governance frameworks if they are properly formulated. They establish guidelines for interacting with interested parties (monitored individuals, banking clients and the public) and shareholders (the government), as well as for establishing internal governance structures that complement external ones. They serve as the foundation for the protocols used to ensure that the agency meets its goals and monitors its effectiveness. While there are few formal allusions to these four pillars in research on commercial governance, there are several obvious connections. For example, the requirement for an arm's length connection between executives and shareholders in the (private) business community is like the regulator's requirement of independence from shareholders as well as other stakeholders (Chiu, 2011). Accountability agreements between executives and proprietors and other stakeholders must be in place for their responsibilities as trustees to be successful. Moreover, integrity safeguards are in place to prevent conflicts between competing interests and transparency systems to help with compliance. One distinction – or point of emphasis – between private nonfinancial enterprises and regulatory authorities is the number of stakeholders, particularly financial supervisors. Therefore, for the purpose of satisfaction and ensured accountability government organizations must be held more accountable than private businesses.

Independence

Quintyn and Taylor (2007) address the benefits and structures underlying financial legislators' independence. The governing body needs to be shielded from inappropriate influence from political parties and from the organizations that it is supervising as a foundation for effective governance. Making meaningful policy commitments will be easier with a decent amount of independence from both sides. Despite that, it is important to remember that agency independence is never completely guaranteed. These 'unelected officials' are an essential component of the government in our democratic systems and must share the government's overarching goals and duties. The fact that independence is recognized as a cornerstone of the governance of regulations rather than as a goal serves to further underscore this crucial concept. The regulatory and administrative elements of the job, or the crucial facets of the responsibilities, should be covered by financial sector officials' independence. In terms of organizational and financial considerations, these two should have a good amount of independence. The external independence measures require approval of certain internal governance components, such as the structure of the governing body or boards, the process by which members are chosen, the roles played by the boards of directors, the voting privileges of the members and the collaborative character of decisions made by the board.

Research on the independence of financial regulation has long dominated the importance of legislative and administrative independence. The necessity for investigations on this kind of independence has grown as recent periods of financial instability and political constraints have placed banking regulation and oversight into the public eye. The true benefits and expenses of having an impartial regulator and supervisor still needed to be considered. It is evident that increased financial stability is correlated with greater regulation and administrative independence. Financial independence still comprises of four types:

Independence of Institution

The agency's standing as a governing body apart from the executive and legislative subparts of government is referred to as institutional independence. The government's ministry of finances is an example of a government agency that usually lacks independence (Pollitt & Talbot, 2003). Three essential components of this type of independence are as follows:

(1) The most effective way to preserve independence is to have well-defined recruitment and dismissal policies that are based mostly on the integrity and competency of regulators. Authorities would have tenure security under such regulations, allowing them to express themselves and act without fear of being fired by the current administration.
(2) The legal framework of the agency. Multi-member committees are not as inclined to be led by the opinions of a single person and help guarantee uniformity and continuity of decision-making across tenure.
(3) Through the decision-generating process's transparency, many judgements inevitably entail sensitive commercial information that would be challenging to reveal. There should be an expectation that decision-making procedures are transparent, allowing both enterprises and the public to examine them closely and reduce potential risks.

Autonomy in Regulations

The ability of an agency to exercise a suitable degree of autonomy in establishing prudential laws and regulations for the industries it oversees, while adhering to legal constraints, is known as regulatory independence. In addition to broad guidelines pertaining to the stability of the company and its operations, prudential regulations also include guidelines derived specifically from the unique characteristics of financial intermediation (Osma et al., 2019). These basic guidelines serve as the foundation for the supervisory process and have a significant effect on the stability of the financial system. To guarantee that the industry adheres to global best standards and practices, a high degree of autonomy in establishing prudential regulations is crucial, as seen from the perspective of regulatory independence.

Autonomy in Supervision

The primary means by which supervisors maintain stable financial systems are licencing, both onsite and remote checks, penalties and the implementation of prohibitions (Barth et al., 2009). Supervisory autonomy pertains to the impartiality that allows the agency to carry out these functions. For the four elements of autonomy, supervisory autonomy is the hardest to ensure, yet being essential to the stability of the financial industry. The role of supervision usually entails private ordering between the supervisor and the supervised institution with the goal of maintaining its efficacy. However, the supervisory process's seclusion leaves it open to manipulation by regulated firms as well as politicians. It is challenging to protect the supervisors from all types of political involvement because it might appear obscure and take many different shapes. Financial autonomy.

Financial Autonomy

The power of the supervisory authority to decide on the amount of its own budget as well as the precise distribution of assets and targets within it is referred to as budgetary autonomy. High budgetary autonomy oversight organizations are better able to resist political influence (which could be applied through budgetary challenges), react faster to developing needs in the field of monitoring and guarantee that earnings are sufficiently appealing for retaining qualified personnel. A supervisory agency that receives funding from the general government budget or from a ministry that oversees its operations is susceptible to political meddling in several ways. For instance, if the regulators are thought to be overly severe on politically connected financial institutions, the government may threaten to withhold financing or to restrict it (Light, 2011). Furthermore, it may have to reduce its funding during periods of budgetary austerity, which frequently corresponds with the escalating issues in the banking sector and calls for more oversight. If there is a general agreement that funding must come from public coffers, the agency will propose and justify the supervisory budget based on impartial standards related to market trends.

These risks are mitigated by funding through a tax on the regulated firms. But if the levy isn't set up correctly, it could give the impression that the business is dependent on the budget. In several countries, the government and the supervisory agency work together to examine the appropriateness of the fees and to prevent industry capture. Fee-based funding is also susceptible to the possibility that during times of industrial stress, the supervisor's resources will be severely constrained. Putting money aside for the agency to use in emergencies like these seems to be the best course of action (Desai, 2011).

Transparency

It is generally accepted that the concept of transparency has a strong connection to governance. It is essential to rebuild trust in the sustainability of the financial infrastructure as a whole. It has a three-dimensional, rule-based strategy achieving in financial governance, acknowledging that markets for financial services are shaped by a multitude of local and global participants, regulations and standards.

An important aspect of transparency is securing financial regulation within the larger legal system. Therefore, the organizations and mechanisms used to regulate the financial markets are defined by this constitutional feature. The too-big-to-fail dilemma that emerged in the wake of the financial crisis is a crucial concern and a great example of capitalism. Financial legislation must specify the relevant processes and institutions that can handle this issue (Garicano & Lastra, 2010). This necessitates a political judgement that must be transparent regardless of how it is expressed. Therefore, from the standpoint of openness, it makes little difference if a nation chooses to adopt a 'technical' strategy by working with the central bank and regulatory institutions, or a 'political' solution by including the legislature in the process. The important thing is that all decisions be made transparently, which increases the system's overall confidence.

The principles and goals of monetary regulation are connected to the second component of transparency. It consists of two components: first, it makes clear the intended objectives and core principles of government financial policy; second, it makes sure that details are easily available and easily understood. The most important factor is information accuracy rather than quantity. Transparency of central bank intentions serves as one example in this regard. Accountability is the third component of transparency as a further crucial component of effective governance. As there are several players in the financial markets and a wide range of norms that apply, it is necessary to approach the issue of guaranteeing responsibility from multiple perspectives. In the financial services industry, transparency is considered more as a reconstitution of procedures and standards than as a reflection of them. Transparency's revolutionary powers seem to be limited to a move away from the emphasis on the veracity of the information supplied and towards bureaucratic process completion. At first, there were conflicting responses to the changes made to the compliance function. While some interviewees saw adherence to transparency requirements as a checklist, others claimed that compliance work required a substantial investment of time. Despite these disparate approaches to compliance, it became clear that standards and business operations were not integrated. Professionals viewed compliance as a distinct task that could be harmful to their firm rather than viewing their procedures and operations as being compatible with worldwide standards. This realization seemed to point to a structural propensity to restrict transparency involvement, forming a flight path established in reaction to global regulatory needs. The effective ring-fenced of companies from compliance processes eliminates the possible transformative abilities of the improved advantageous ownership transparency administration if the primary objective of luminous arrangements is to influence the practices and behaviours of those subject to transparency regulations. Professionals' level of participation with transparency requirements is severely limited by practices that include outsourced legal processes to additional agencies, governments or empowered personnel.

The banking sector can benefit from blockchain technology, which emphasizes decentralization and the use of AI algorithms to facilitate safe and transparent processes. Big Data is essential to the financial industry because it combines enormous databases and AI techniques to produce insights that are actionable, improve decision-making and improve operational effectiveness. Massive amounts of financial data are effectively managed by AI-driven analytics, allowing for immediate decision-making, evaluation of risks and predictive modelling for better financial results. AI-based industries have benefited from technological advancement, and more institutions are joining the competition. Either they are paying billions to acquire AI talent or insurance companies and banks are turning out AI competence. By incorporating machine learning (ML) into trading methods, managing risks and choices regarding investments, it has greatly increased market effectiveness and return on investments.

Accountability

Accountability and independence are complementary, in other words, accountability systems can support agency independence. As a result, the idea of a 'trade-off' between independence and accountability is erroneous in as much as it implies that a regulatory body with stronger accountability measures would obviously be less autonomous.

On the other hand, weak transparency for accountability or 'control' mechanisms passing for accountability mechanisms are a real problem that the concept of trade-offs helps to detect. A good example of one that undermines administrative independence and will eventually be inconsistent with it is one that grants the minister of finance the power to step in and influence agency outcomes in terms of decision making.

The key to creating an accountability system that will promote agency independence is to build a network of overlapping and complementary checking mechanisms. By employing such a combination of arrangements, the intention is to reach a state in which the agency is 'under control,' even while no one is in control of it. Regulatory agencies operate in a multiple-principals environment, which means that accountability to numerous principals will be engaged for each dimension of independence. This makes the creation of such a network of complementary checking mechanisms possible. The governing bodies, the business world and the public (financial institutions clients) are the key players. The greatest method to make sure that accountability systems don't compromise independence is to follow the openness principle. It serves to strengthen public trust in the banking supervisor and promotes transparent administration. Openness is achieved by means of yearly reports, press briefings, knowledge events and the release of all laws and regulations, management procedures and significant decisions. These are usually posted on the agency's website (McDermott, 2010). There are çomparable aspects of accountability that may be found for each of the four tiers of independence.

The Accountability of Institution

As a result of its representational nature, the legislative process is essential to the supervision of executive branch operations in most political systems. Ensuring that public policy is implemented in line with the intent of legislation is the goal of its supervision. A committee formed by the legislature is the body to which the regulatory agency is accountable in most jurisdictions that have set up a system of accountability to the lawmakers.[2] This gives parliamentarians the opportunity to become knowledgeable about the intricate financial and technological matters that the regulatory body handles. A higher level of continuity for the purpose of monitoring can also be guaranteed via panels. The agency's executive director may typically be called before these panels to give evidence or provide reports.

[2]https://www.elibrary.imf.org/display/book/9781589060432/ch007.xml

The accounting supervisor's official supervisory body in several nations is the ministry of finances; nonetheless, this kind of accountability arrangement may cast doubt on the supervisor's impartiality. There exists a narrow boundary separating the exercise of political power from reporting and dialogs. There should be no involvement on the part of the ministry in operational or policy choices. It is easy for oversight to turn into a tool for political pressure to be applied to the agency. Ongoing reporting by the supervising agency and the option for the president to inquire about information or hold talks with the regulatory body are the kinds of accountability systems that would seem most compatible with agency autonomy.

Accountability in Regulations

A regulatory body that is tasked with creating rules must be held responsible for how it uses that power. Since legislators would typically delegate the supervisory agency's rule-making capabilities, one of the primary subjects of the reporting to the legislative branch that was previously discussed must be the exercise of this authority (Yackee & Yackee, 2016). Accountability to parliament also offers a chance for a discussion on the quality of the legal framework, in which the agency should be able to raise any issues with its oversight procedures that could be addressed through legislative amendments, since parliament also has the final say over changing the legal foundation upon which the agency operates.

Accountability in Supervision

The judiciary's review is a fundamental component of regulatory bodies' accountability relationships concerning supervisory measures, especially considering the broad legal authority bestowed upon them (Athanassiou, 2011). Any autonomous organization needs to answer the people whose lives are impacted by its choices. The latter ought to be able to seek legal recourse in a court of law. Through the process of judicial review, the courts can monitor how public power is used. The judicial review of administrative actions has historically been used to make sure the decision-maker is acting within the bounds of authority. It pertains to the procedure as well as, occasionally, albeit to a reduced degree, the result. It is widely acknowledged that those who are impacted by an agency's decisions, whether as individuals or institutions, have the right to request an administrative appeal of those judgements. To uphold natural justice, the agency must adhere to several due process standards when making decisions, including granting, or denying licences and applying penalties. The person to whom a formal decision has been addressed must be made aware of their legal options as soon as possible. These specifications are meant to guarantee that the process is as open and transparent as feasible, and that a reasonable and equitable judgement is reached.

In addition, judicial review reviews the case's merits and facts and confirms that the findings reached by the court are lawful. The challenge here is that an administrator is usually granted a great deal of privacy, and legal systems generally exercise constraint and defer to the supervisor's expertise because they are typically not financial experts and are therefore hesitant to impose their judgement on supervisors. As a result, substantive accountability is given less weight, and judicial review is typically restricted to examining legality to make sure that discretion is not being used improperly or in bad faith. In order to prevent judicial review from impeding the efficacy and efficiency of regulation and supervision and ultimately undermining agency autonomy, it must be restricted and time limited.

Financial Accountability

The visualization of financial records, which show the periodicity of the expenditures, is a crucial tool for agency accountability. However, this accountability feature shouldn't be used as a covert means of compromising agency independence. The foundation of independence is the agency's ability to make decisions on its priorities and financial requirements on its own. Financial accountability should typically be restricted to past budgetary accountability, concentrating on an independent the accountant's examination of the yearly accounts and reconciliations to assess whether appropriate financial administration has been carried out, whether the governing body is effectively allocating its finances, and whether the financial statements accurately reflect the situation. This helps to preserve agency autonomy.

Integrity

The fundamental principle of integrity is frequently overlooked. Nonetheless, it is crucial since it offers a number of foundations for sound internal governance which reinforce external influences. Integrity is the collection of controls that guarantee agency employees can work towards institutional objectives without jeopardizing them out of their own interests or behaviour. Employees of regulatory organizations are impacted by integrity on many levels. The nomination procedures, periods of office and termination criteria of directors should be designed to protect the integrity of the board-level appointments (policy making body). Furthermore, the internal inspection procedures guarantee that the organization's objectives are precisely defined, followed and accountability is upheld. This preserves the integrity of the agency's everyday activities (Ismail, 2013).

Maintaining the agency's operational excellence will uphold the organization's integrity and increase its trustworthiness with the public. Third, in order to avoid conflicts of interest, integrity also suggests that officials and staff members must follow certain rules when it comes to their personal lives. Fourth, maintaining integrity also means that regulatory agency employees are legally protected while performing their official tasks. Lacking legislative safeguards, employees' impartiality would be vulnerable to attack or corruption, and the reputation of the organization and general efficacy would be negatively impacted.

Governance in the Financial Services Industry

Corporate governance plays a key role in ensuring the stability, integrity and reputation of financial institutions within the complex fabric of the financial sector; effective governance is not just about compliance requirements; They are key to these organizations' sustainable growth and risk management.

The Importance of Corporate Governance in Financial Institutions

Corporate governance in financial institutions includes the policies, principles and procedures for directing and managing corporations. The ultimate goal is to align the interests of individuals, companies and the public as evenly as possible. For financial institutions, strong governance is important for several reasons:

- The management of financial institutions should make available the general approach for managing operational risks in a way that makes it easy for stakeholders and investors to assess the bank's effectiveness in detecting, assessing, mitigating and controlling operational risks. Operational risk should be assessed to ensure that it aligns with the bank's present operations, business plans and rules. Senior management can make sure that an independent, skilled, informed staff member conducts an efficient and thorough internal audit of the bank's operational risk management system. In order to guarantee that branches are adequately informed of the protocols and laws pertaining to the internal surveillance system and managing operational risks, the upper management of banks ought to liaison collaboration between the internal auditor and risk administration department.
- Legal advice on compliance can, in the near term, save costs and increase the earnings of financial services companies. New compliance solutions eventually surface because of financial services organizations competing with one another. The financial services industry can now cope with more regulation because of these technologies, which also reduce compliance costs. Financial firms bear the price of this growing regulatory burden. Financial institutions can become more globally competitive through an expanding compliance and regulatory industry.
- Another aspect to ensure strong governance is to improve the overall performance of the financial framework. There must be a very justifiable and logical framework that helps in decision-making through an authentic process. All the activities must be executed effectively in compliance with the institution's proposed objectives.
- One of the most important reasons is to gain the trust of the stakeholders involved. It supports financial stability and inclusivity, which in turn promotes economic progress. Without trust, banks are unable to draw in depositors or locate homes ready to take out loans to fund their residences and companies.

Governance Framework Modifications in Response to Market and Technological Developments

Financial industry is evolving quickly by technological integrations and getting more digital. Almost every business has been impacted by this change, and the banking sector is no exception. Consumers now anticipate the same degree of accessibility and ease from banking services as they do from other internet businesses. For banking institutions to stay competitive and meet these expectations, they need to go through a digital transformation.

Employers need to train their staff on how to use these resources and get the most out of them. Caution must be used to avoid several serious mistakes, one of which is the attempt to establish causality by association. Financial institutions may better understand what their clients want, how they can customize their financial solutions to meet those needs and how to reach out to them through marketing by providing answers to five crucial questions. To find the answers to these questions, data analytics must be used to extract new insights from the available data.

But it's important to keep in mind that no matter how advanced an analytics tool is, it won't guarantee success. Employers need to train their staff on how to use these resources and get the most out of them. Caution must be used to avoid several serious mistakes, one of which is the attempt to establish causality by association. A significant part in finance and accounting is played by data science. It can increase profitability and competitiveness by enabling accountants to produce more precise and in-depth projections. With ever-increasing volumes of data at our disposal, forecast accuracy is developing thanks in large part to big data and predictive analytics. As of right now, organizations face difficulties when it comes to predicting with big data because standard technologies are unable to process data of the scale, speed and complexity present.

Cases of Successful and Failed Governance

Significant insight into the beneficial effects of governance on economic growth can be gained by examining empirical case studies of successful and poor governance. The FSB noted several inadequacies in the board's risk governance assessment, such as the shareholders' lack of understanding of intricate financial issues, their reluctance to challenge top management and their disdain for risk management protocols. A few boards did not contribute sufficiently to the development and execution of risk management procedures.

A few financial firms, like Lehman Brothers and United Bank of Switzerland, restricted the board's ability to control risk management practices (Ellul, 2015). In several establishments, the risk management department lacked the necessary degree of competence. Furthermore, the management of UBS failed to sufficiently identify and assess risks. The board and top management were not informed of the institution's risk exposures, which was another problem. Inadequate reporting lines made it more difficult for the board to supervise. Risks were frequently dependent on activities rather than being evaluated at the firm-wide level. In the

2008 Shareholders Report on UBS's write-downs, the large Swiss bank UBS admitted without delay to the shortcomings of the risk management procedure (UBS, 2008). The significant failures in governance, risk management, risk controls and payment system are acknowledged by UBS in the same official document. In that way UBS successfully redesign the process with the goal of preventing similar failures.

International investments bank Goldman Sachs has embraced an extensive ecological strategy that recognizes the importance of ecological services and is supporting the establishment of an innovative Centre for Environmental Markets to increase the incorporation of social and environmental factors into investment and lending operations.

The financial services sector lacks consistency in its governance. It is a dynamic, ever-evolving process that must adjust to new market trends, technological advancements and regulatory frameworks. Since sound governance is the cornerstone upon which financial institutions' stability, integrity, and reputation are built, its significance cannot be emphasized. Organizations can ensure resilience by updating and refining their governance structures based on lessons learnt from prior successes and failures.

Emerging Trends and Their Implications for Regulation and Governance

The administrative operations' internationalization has also been expedited by technology. Offshoring administrative duties has been popular for several decades. A lot of financial companies moved customer service and call centres to less expensive locations first, then IT operations and application handling. The emergence of cloud computing has expedited this trend. These days, entire IT systems, including central banking systems, can be hosted globally. Certain products and services may even be provided entirely outside of the borders of the customer's nation in areas with shared regulatory frameworks. Furthermore, fintech companies have an abundance of innovative opportunities when it comes to providing financial services, given the ever-evolving preferences and habits of their clients about the use of new technology in the financial sector.

This is not an uncommon trend; for several years, major financial institutions have been using technology to increase productivity. By utilizing cutting-edge technology, banks are attempting to push the envelope and maintain a personal connection with their clients. With an emphasis on user-centric features and functionalities, third-party payment systems such as Paytm, Mobikwik and others are effectively fulfilling their roles (Sundar & Suguna, 2024). And in the world of finance, mobile devices continue to be revolutionary. Jobs in banking are being rapidly replaced by automation, and the skill sets needed in the finance industry are changing as well.

Upgrading outdated core systems will become essential in the future. The financial industry's infrastructure was put to the test and its established mechanisms were challenged by the events of 2020. For instance, during the COVID-19 epidemic, many core systems were unable to process the volume of transactions that came through. As a result, outdated systems found it difficult to handle the increased demands. Business decisions driven by data are not limited to e-commerce. The financial industry is also seeing a trend of utilizing data analytics technology. Data analytics is being used by financial institutions to enhance client satisfaction and obtain a competitive advantage over their rivals. Banks are concentrating on employing data analytics approaches to significantly increase their performance and efficiency. Soon, professionals with relevant expertise and a certification in data analytics will have great employment opportunities in the banking industry.

Cryptocurrencies, Decentralised Finance (DeFi), Regulatory Technology (RegTech) and Central Bank Digital Currencies (CBDCs) are the emerging trends introduced. FinTech companies have emerged as a result of the expansion of Digital Finance and Digital Money (DFDM) in the financial fields.[3] Financial Technology (FinTech) enterprises enable a wide range of financial goods, financial businesses, finance-related software and new forms of client interaction and communication that fall under the umbrella of DFDM. A further rising trend is the increasing number of businesses and customers gravitating towards financial products and payments based on blockchain technology, sometimes referred to as cryptocurrencies. Cryptography protects this digital or virtual cash, making it nearly hard to replicate or use twice.

With the advent of new digital tools, reporting is easier and more rapid. Because of advanced analytics, technological advancements are allowing shareholders to get data in real time. Financial firms have long used data analytics to help customers obtain insightful information, spot areas for process enhancements or assist organizations in better risk management. However, organizations may now leverage ML and AI to enable improved data, supporting more sophisticated analytics and real-time insight delivery through data visualization tools.

The immediate accessibility of system resources, or cloud companies, are rapidly being integrated into the financial infrastructure despite typically existing outside of legal bounds. This is because cloud computing offers financial companies' advantages of scale, adaptability, affordability and efficiency in operations, all of which are making them more and more reliant on it. However, cloud services come with drawbacks, including concentration risk, cyberattack security concerns, data protection, financial secrecy and disruptions. Because so many institutions rely on big cloud providers, they run the risk of developing a single point of breakdown, which has an impact on both individual enterprises and the systemic level. Administrators specifying access and audit privileges are necessary due to the uncontrolled nature of cloud providers and their frequent location in third-world nations. This creates additional regulatory challenges. Growing data localization regulations are making it harder for data to move across borders, which raises expenses and, paradoxically, makes regulatory control more difficult.

[3]https://www.elibrary.imf.org/view/journals/063/2023/011/article-A001-en.xml

Big data and IoT usage are closely intertwined. Financial companies can use data, which is gathered from possibly numerous devices (such as smart phones, bank ATMs and biometric detectors), to predict client demands, offer individualized solutions and even potentially detect fraud. The use of smartphone apps in cars to transmit data on driving performance and guide underwriting decisions is a well-known example in the insurance industry. Data can assist companies in gaining market share by enabling them to provide better, more competitive services. Financial services such as banking, capital markets and managing investments have potential applications.

Although blockchain first gained notoriety as the technology underlying bitcoin, its potential is considerably greater as it gains significance. Use cases for cryptoassets aside include trading purposes, managing assets, verification of identity, clearance and development, DeFi, and accountability. A lot of use cases rely on 'smart contract' technology, which makes it possible to automate certain types of transactions (like payments) when specific requirements are satisfied. Another example of the technology is non-fungible tokens, or NFTs, which are unique and non-transferable units of data that can represent ownership in and facilitate trading of any kind of unique item, whether it be tangible or intangible (e.g. art, music, films and collectibles). Blockchain development has been hampered by legal uncertainty, but this is starting to change.

A significant technological breakthrough in 2023 was Generative AI (Feuerriegel et al., 2024). The financial industry was significantly altered by this development. This year, FinTech – such as apps and other online money services – is anticipated to have a greater impact on fintech and the application of generative AI to chatbots, potentially creating new revenue streams. It provides access to a whole new range of innovations that may be used to customize investment management and financial planning. Insurance is one area where this is evident. AI assists insurers in developing customized solutions by identifying patterns in data, which may result in more precise risk assessments and lower insurance prices for individuals.

The enormous impact that technology currently has in the financial sector will need to be taken into consideration by finance experts. Considering evolving consumer tastes and practices. Banks and other financial institutions must assess the value of their business activities as they attempt to become increasingly technologically flexible.

The Challenges of Emerging Trends

To be competitive and meet consumer demands in the rapidly changing digital environment of today, financial services providers need to make system improvements. The strategic importance of digital financial institutions in their local economies is increasing. Often referred to as Neobanks, they suffer a greater risk than the conventional banks that originate from consumer lending, which is typically less protected against losses due to its higher degree of uncollateralization. Their vulnerability also includes increased risk-taking in the securities they hold, and increased hazards associated with liquidity (i.e. the proportion of liquid assets maintained by neobanks to deposits is typically lower than that for conventional banks). Regulators encounter additional challenges during economic downturns because the risk management procedures and overall stability of most Neobanks are unverified. FinTech businesses exert pressure on more established rivals in the financial services industry in addition to investing in greater risks among themselves (Varma et al., 2022). As a case study, the United States can be investigated, where FinTech mortgage representatives adopt an aggressive growth strategy during periods of increased home financing, such as during the pandemic. It is anticipated that the competitive pressure from FinTech companies will continue to negatively impact the profitability of traditional financial institutions.

DeFi is yet another innovation that has expanded quickly over the last years. It is a monetary network built on cryptocurrency that operates without the need for a central middleman. Known by another name, DeFi, it has the capacity to provide financial services that are more inventive, inclusive and transparent because of its increased accessibility and efficiency. DeFi, however, also entails the accumulation of leverage and is especially susceptible to hazards related to the market, liquidity and cyberspace. Cyberattacks are often fatal for these sites, taking financial assets and eroding user confidence. They can be rather serious for traditional banks as well. The idea that all deposits are at risk is reinforced by DeFi's absence of deposit insurance. In the past, announcements of provider cyberattack were frequently followed by substantial client withdrawals. FinTech brings more than just competition, even though they are entering the market to compete with traditional banks on an even playing field. As a matter of fact, banks continue to provide FinTechs with leverage and liquidity, which keeps the two entwined.

Financial regulators encounter challenges from administrative arbitrage, where businesses move or set up shop in less closely watched industries and regions and collaboration, which may require oversight and regulatory actions, such as better protection for investors and consumers. It is necessary to have regulations that target FinTech startups and traditional banks equally. This way, the potential that FinTech offers is fostered and dangers are controlled. Neobanks must consequently adhere to stronger capital, liquidity and risk-management norms commensurate with their risks. The well-being of less technologically sophisticated banks may require more careful business supervision from traditional financial institutions and other developed enterprises, as their current business models may not be as long-term viable.

Due to the absence of regulatory agencies, DeFi poses a challenge to effective regulation and monitoring. Legislation in this case should focus on the organizations – like centralized cryptocurrency exchanges and stablecoin issuers – that are driving the explosive expansion of DeFi. Strong governance, such as self-regulatory groups and industry norms, should be promoted by supervisory authorities.

Core Advantages of Emerging Trends

The financial industry is dynamic and ever evolving, with new trends in the field developing on a regular basis. Nearly every industry globally is undergoing a digital revolution but banks in particular stand to gain greatly from the following ways that digital transformation of key processes might occur:

- In contemporary tech-heavy environment, where consumers demand ever-faster outcomes, digitalization is essential to grow customers and compete in any industry. Customers that expect quick and easy online banking options rather than slow and laborious traditional banking are among those with higher expectations.
- Efficiency is essential in a society where accuracy and quickness are highly valued. Modern banking processes are now lot faster and simpler thanks to sophisticated digital analytics. The digital transformation has an impact on daily banking activities such as electronic signatures that don't require physical the printing process, on-the-go approvals for loans that don't require visiting a loan office, automated bill pay that makes sure clients aren't behind on their monthly payments, contributions, and transfers via smartphone apps.
- Any management team's ability to gather knowledge will improve their ability to make wise judgements. Data drive the most important decisions, and digitalization assists financial institutions in making those difficult but informed decisions by providing precise, up-to-date data that best serve consumer demands.
- Compared to traditional money exchange methods, digital transformation requires fewer continuing financial investments, which enhances long-term cost efficiency. Digitalization, for instance, has reduced the cost of using middlemen to transfer physical cash between parties by increasing accessibility and streamlining online transactions without cash.
- In modern financial services and banking industries, consolidations and acquisitions are almost inevitable. Compatibility issues have historically resulted from merging companies with different physical systems, which can be disastrous for both IT departments involved. On the other hand, cloud-based solutions eliminate the need for on-site systems, enabling a more seamless digital merger of corporate units.
- Banks can transition from their old systems – which are frequently a patchwork of incompatible technologies that miscommunicate data – to a more user-friendly centralized system by utilizing digital transformation. Numerous benefits stem from this shift, such as more streamlined and compact bank technology stacks, less costly and time-consuming maintenance, standardized data throughout the financial institution, enhanced data quality and reduced or eliminated time-consuming data transformation procedures.
- The availability of consolidated, real-time data more instantly enhances banks' capacity to process reports with greater speed and accuracy. Financial institutions can monitor evolving patterns, respond quickly and identify issues at the outset. Senior management may now create reports independently that would have otherwise required IT resources to assemble and format thanks to these additional insights. Considering these reports take less time and labour to produce, banks can assign the staff members who were previously in charge of gathering these data to more analytical positions that have a bigger impact on the company's operations.

- Financial institutions can use automated compliance monitoring tools through digital financial management solutions. Banks are therefore able to allocate fewer resources to audits. By automatically standardizing and delivering data from old applications into the new platform, the risks associated with manual inputs can be reduced. Additionally, since these digitalized cloud-based systems receive frequent compliance updates, the bank won't have to deal with any new or amended rules.

Open Issues and the Future of Regulation and Governance

Even with all the research being done on financial intelligence, more work needs to be done to create a more sophisticated solution that satisfies inclusive finance standards. It is acknowledged that AI-powered finance will exist in the future, with a multi-agent AI system serving as the foundation for financial transactions and AI agents becoming more logical decision makers than humans. Explainable financial agents and causation, perception and prediction under uncertainty, risk-sensitive and robust decision-making, and multi-agent game and mechanism design are critical technological difficulties that must be addressed to realize FinTech in the era of improved AI. These unresolved problems and potential paths forward may serve as the basis for the advancement of AI in the finance industry.

The ability to justify judgements, forecasts and suggestions is a critical competency of financial agents. But the computational techniques that are in use today typically produce forecasts that are opaque to individuals and hardly ever provide a meaningful explanation of the decision-making process. To create explainable agents, causal inference must be provided to comprehend the real world and encourage interactive diagnostic evaluation that is dependable and evaluate the relevance of a characteristic by replaying a forecast against previously disturbed inputs. Perceptions and predictions-based AI agents that facilitates financial insights and indicate what is going to occur next ought to be process insufficient data and record temporal correlation sequences under ambiguity given the dynamic nature of economic conditions. To further enhance the financial intelligent services, major financial applications including risk administration, identity authorization and market surveillance should use these intelligent perception and prediction techniques.

The financial agents must be threat-sensitive and resilient to defects and ambiguity to perform well in mission-critical applications like risk management and portfolio selection. There are two ways to approach this problem. One way to address this issue is by developing source-specific noise models that can detect the historical origin of data automatically and can identify the relative importance of various data sources using confidence ranges. However, in the worst-case situation, risk-sensitive decision models can also be built that include risk considerations in loss estimators and optimization techniques. Supply chains, investors, internet-based resources and logistics are all part of the financial markets that constitute multi-agent systems. Designing trading mechanisms, dynamic pricing of assets, supply chain management and reliable banking systems all depend on knowing how to play multi-agent games. A strong financial incentive system that accurately reflects the fluctuations of supply and demand in everyday life is required to accomplish price dynamics. To balance platforms profits and customer satisfaction, e-commerce sites can also be developed to explore various interests and find an appropriate balance in the game of clients, businesses and recommendation-based AI-bots.

Incentives and cooperative activities need to be measured. The possible future of economic AI, in which AI agents exchange business with humans, companies and other AI agents, has also been the subject of extensive study. To create the norms of interaction for AI agent's in the future economic system, the creation of rational agents, or 'machina economicus', must be launched.

Summary

This concluding chapter offers an in-depth investigation of the emerging and existing facets of financial governance and legislation. The financial system's framework and the crucial role that regulation plays in guaranteeing stability and integrity are covered in its initial sections. It also presents the rapid pace of the revolution in the finance industry and how it has compelled regulatory bodies to adjust and evolve. These legal regulations strengthen the financial sector by addressing risks related to stability, transparency and customer protection while embracing the advantages of innovation. Additionally, the importance of corporate governance in financial institutions is highlighted. The discussion addresses the values that support effective risk management, accountability in terms of compliance and trust of the stakeholders. The discussion examines the responsibilities of key participants, including panels, executives, owners and legislators, to investigate how these concepts are implemented. Investigated the complexities and challenges of governance, with an emphasis on globally linked financial institutions.

Furthermore, certain governance framework modifications in response to market and technological developments are also needed. To sustain the state-of-the-art technological modifications, employers need to train their staff on how to use these resources and get the most out of them. Caution must be used to avoid several serious mistakes, one of which is the attempt to establish causality by association. A significant part in finance and accounting is also played by data science. Some organizations faced difficulties when it comes to predicting with big data because standard technologies are unable to process data of the scale, speed and complexity present. The financial industry is undergoing an incredible phase, and it can be clearly observed that in daily lives it has been modified how the bills are paid to use banking services. This phase introduces technological trends including hybrid cloud computing, data science, generative AI, cybersecurity risk management, sustainability, open banking and digital currencies. Additionally, given is a summary of the intricate conceptual and practical obstacles emerging market economies must overcome to overhaul their finance regulatory regimes. These economies are trying to strike a compromise between the demands of improved financial inclusiveness, growth and the ultimate objective of financial stability. These goals might support one another. Components of cross-border regulations and macroeconomic strategies that affect financial stability and the robustness of the financial sector in emerging economies are also considered. Any potential prejudices and the requirement for ethical artificial intelligence practices in making financial choices have been brought to light by studies investigating the moral consequences of AI and big data in economics. The combination of big data and ML in finance may give rise to legal difficulties, including those related to data privacy, algorithmic transparency and the dynamic regulatory environment.

Despite the numerous emerging technologies in the financial sector there are still open issues and future recommendations specifically related to regulation and governance. Even with all the research being done on financial intelligence, more work needs to be done to create a more sophisticated solution that satisfies inclusive finance standards. Today's computational methods almost never offer a meaningful explanation of the decision-making process and usually result in forecasts that are opaque to individuals. To develop explainable agents, causal inference – which assesses the importance of a characteristic by replaying a forecast against previously disturbed inputs – must be made available to understand the real world and promote interactive diagnostic evaluation that is trustworthy. E-commerce sites can also be built to investigate different interests and establish an optimal balance in the game of customers, businesses and recommendation-based AI-bots to balance platform revenues and customer satisfaction.

Learning Objectives

(1) Understand the Evolving Role of Regulation and Governance in Financial Systems.
(2) Develop the connection between emerging financial development and regulatory framework.
(3) Evaluate the adaptation and responsiveness of regulatory and governance models.
(4) Gain insight into the future of economic policy and governance.

Chapter 10

Quantum Computing and Its Implications for Financial Markets

Introduction of Quantum Computer

The history of financial services dates back to the era where employing physics to figure out tough and complex issues was used. The model of Black Scholes Merton framework, for instance, applies the Brownian motion approach for pricing of financial instruments such as call options in Europe throughout the duration (Derman & Miller, 2016; Lee, 2018).

Utilizing innovative quantum advancement for financial estimations and answering queries, particularly to survive uncertainty and handle artificial optimization, is considered to be one of the biggest benefit for initial-users. Quantum computers have the capability to conduct estimations which provide 'Dynamic Arbitrage Opportunities' ignored by rivals. In addition, they provide enhance adherence, leveraging behavioural information to improve service provided to customers, and prompt reaction to market instability (Herman et al., 2022). These are few of the particular advantages anticipated from quantum computers.

The main benefit of quantum-computers is the 'Solution-space' compared to binary computers regardless their sturdiness (Möller & Vuik, 2017). It is due to the higher power which is double the power of basic computers needed regarding multiplying the transistors number working on an issue. The quantum-computing power could be around twice every time just single qubit is included.

Quantum computing can further allow financial amenities to re-structure operational procedures, for example (i) decision in back and front office regarding client management for 'Know your customer', orientation and credit underwriting, (ii) management of treasury and assets as well as trading and (iii) optimization of firms, comprising management of compliance and risk.[1,2]

---

[1]https://www.adlittle.com/en/insights/report/unleashing-business-potential-quantum-computing

[2]https://www.financierworldwide.com/closer-than-you-think-quantum-computing-in-finance

---

The Global Evolution, Changing Landscape and Future of Financial Markets, 119–131
Copyright © 2025 Syed Ali Raza, Darakhshan Syed, Syed Rizwan and Maiyra Ahmed
Published under exclusive licence by Emerald Publishing Limited
doi:10.1108/978-1-83549-330-420251010

Specifications of quantum computing regarding financial facilitation can be categorized into following classes: (a) prediction and targeting, (b) optimization of trading, (c) profiling of risk. Quantum computing offers possible utilization scenarios in every class, like in financial amenities named insurance, banking and financial markets (Albareti et al., 2022).

According to Hassija et al. (2020), quantum mechanical phenomena are supported by quantum computers in order to control and manage data, via depending on quantum qubits or bits. This kind of innovation and advancement estimations are highly effectively when working on probability distribution, data mapping, samples evaluation and recapitulating. Further, these computers allow for exponential power to solve arithmetically complex numerical, enhancing precision, reducing runtimes of computations and handling past difficult estimations (Chauhan et al., 2022).

In today's era financial amenity users require modified and personalized facilities which promptly comprehend their changing demands and expectations (Crittenden et al., 2019). Financial institutions labelled as small- and medium-sized lose their customer base around 25% because of providing them the facilities or products which are not customer-based or customer-centric. This is challenging to form an analytic framework which examines behavioural data and mounds it speedily and precisely sufficient to select which services or products are required by particular users in almost real time. Additionally, this issue limits financial institutions from offering prompt and personalized services as well product solutions, letting go of the chance to increase their present customer base and target the 1.7 billion adults globally who do not have a bank account.[3]

A subsequent issue persists in detection of fraud. This is analyzed that financial institutions are recurring loss of around 10 to 40 billion USD in earnings within a single year because of below the par management of data and fraud practices. Detection of fraud practices is greatly defective, returning 18% positive false, leading financial institutions to be highly risk averse. In order to assist and make sure precise scoring of credit, the users induction procedure can be prolonged up to 12 weeks. Presently, 70% of banking operations are performed virtually, users prefer those systems and channels which take less time and are efficient.[4] Financial institutions when take more time to communicate efficiently with customers are losing them to those businesses which are customer-centric and within less time satisfy their customers.

For expanding customer-based and enhanced forecasting models, quantum computing can be a ground-breaking innovation (Mosteanu & Faccia, 2021). The data modelling abilities of quantum computers are determined to maintain higher-ranking in identifying trends, conducting categorization and forecasting which are not practical currently due to the difficulties of complicated data networks.

---

[3]https://www.mckinsey.com/industries/financial-services/our-insights/how-quantum-computing-could-change-financial-services

[4]https://cointelegraph.com/explained/how-does-quantum-computing-impact-the-finance-industry

Financial markets are observed to suffer from higher complexity. For instance, the derivatives valuation adjustment framework, the XVA umbrella has highly elevated in complexity, presently comprising debit (DVA), capital (KVA), credit (CVA), margin (MVA) and funding (FVA). As in accordance with higher transparency necessities from rules and regulations, rigorous validation procedures are employed to trading, influencing calculations of risk management which requires to line up credit exposure of counterparty along with credit restriction utilization of derivatives portfolio. Additionally, important financing models and assets have transformed. For instance, ETFs (bond exchange-traded funds) are forecasted to upsurge by 2 trillion USD till 2024, and ESG financing (environment, social and government) are griping with 35 trillion USD financed in the assets taxonomy during 2019.[5]

In this complex landscape of trading, financing managers strive to integrate real-life limitations, named as volatility with market and life-changing events of customer, into the optimization of portfolio. Usually, portfolio managers would indulge to simulate greater number of probable situations and financing alternative to confirm sensitivities when calculating projected returns. In today's era balancing portfolios for financing which matches with movements of markets is considerably unimaginable due to computational restrictions and cost of transactions.

Quantum computing provides assistance in terms of getting through the difficulties of current trading situations. The combinational optimization of quantum computing abilities can assist financing managers to enhance diversification of portfolio, balance investments within portfolios to elevated accuracy reactions to market environment and financiers target and greater cost-effectiveness modernize trading settlement procedures.[6]

Quantum computers assist handle present trading issues. Quantum computers' combinational optimization helps portfolio managers to enhance portfolio via diversification to better allocate funds and plan a balanced portfolio to combat market fluctuations along with streamline trading settlement procedure for cost-effectiveness (Magnuson, 2018).

The financial institutions are under the rock to equalize risk, position of hedging with greater efficiency and conduct a broader range of distress assessment to align with the requirement of regulators (Nielsen & Chuang, 2010). It is difficult to actually manage the expenses associated with risk on swaps since managing liquidity, pricing derivatives, and quantifying risk are all complex processes that are hard to evaluate accurately. Presently, the simulation of Monte Carlo is the widely used approach to examine the effect of volatility and risk in financial modelling which are restricted via estimation error scaling (Bennett & Brassard, 2020).

---

[5]https://www.ibm.com/thought-leadership/institute-business-value/en-us/report/exploring-quantum-financial

[6]https://www.hewwest.com/featured-insights/the-rise-of-quantum-computing

Financial institutions are struggling to balance risk, enhance hedging strategies and conduct overall distress evaluation as well as compliance with law requirements. Pricing derivatives, handling liquidity and assessing risk are difficult tasks with complicated computations, turning it difficult to accurately handle risk-costs in trading. Presently, the most commonly employed technique for evaluating the effect of volatility and risk in financial modelling is Monte Carlo simulation; however, it has shortcomings because of computation errors (Loizou & French, 2012).

Work on Quantum Computing

Various financial activities, from optimization of portfolio to pricing of securities and derivatives, possess the capability needed to evaluate the extent of probable results. In this era, the banking sector is applying models and algorithms which compute probabilities (Bouland et al., 2020). These are moderately efficient yet these are not perfect, as portrayed at the time of financial turmoil years ago, when allegedly few-possible crisis happened more rapidly than projected.

In world with huge data, more robust computing machines are necessary to compute exact possibilities or probabilities. Considering the notion that various financial institutions are willing to adopt an advance generation processor, which operates on quantum physics fundamentals to decode the massive level of information at high speed, the most prominent in the field named 'Google' revealed that Sycamore quantum processor usually takes more than or equal to 180 seconds to complete the activity which can take years for super-computers to perform the same task. The trail efficiently exhibited potential of quantum computers which presently is unimaginable.

Financial markets and institutions which can exploit quantum computers are more likely to emphasize on its considerable advantages. Specifically, they will be capable to efficiently examine huge data sets which are unstructured. Distinct understanding into these segments can assist financial markets as well as institutions to take best possible decision and enhance services provided to customers, for instance via relevant schemes or well-timed announcement of projects. There are evenly high-powered use scenarios in corporate finance, management of portfolios, capital markets and activities related to encryption. In a frequently commoditized atmosphere, it can be a track towards competitive edge. Quantum computers are specifically positive where algorithms are charged via data streams, for example prices of equity in real time which includes a higher degree of noise randomly.

The influence of pandemic has exhibited that the exact and on-time evaluation of risk stays a crucial issue for financial markets and institutions. Although, earlier the happenings of 2020, the past years have witnessed economic and financial catastrophes which cause frequent deviation in how institutions and market stakeholders analyze, price and risk dissimilar asset categories. It drives the initiation of elevating difficulties and real-time risk framework energized via AI however still operational on fundamental computers.

According to Albareti et al. (2022), quantum computers can answer particular queries which are not workable on basic hardware, increasing the power offered via quantum computers and hence has the possibility to transform any sector which utilizes calculation, comprising finance. Initially, applications of quantum computers for the financial sector include simulation, machine learning (ML) and optimization of issues which have previously been offered and employed to uses scenarios like management of portfolio, pricing and management of risk. However, the platforms, algorithms and use scenarios of quantum computers for numerous uses in finance within a structured manner are yet to be explored. It is intended at employees employed in the financial sector aids to earn understanding of the present transformation and abilities and insight the possibility of quantum-computers within the financial sector.

Further, the application of quantum computers to solve financial issues along with the present techniques indicates that the quantum computer's use in algorithm optimization and depicted its use for portfolio optimization, searching for opportunities for arbitrage and credit scoring. It is observed that quantum computers amplitude computations can help in various presently use financial models and techniques due to its high speed (Orús et al., 2019).

In the similar context, Egger et al. (2020) discussed the capability and use of quantum computers for financial queries, focusing on algorithms, optimization, ML and simulation of quantum computers. As per the analysis, quantum-computing advantages are more likely to bring revolution in the financial institutions, which will enhance financial services for customers.

The revolution of financial markets includes fintech technology, which has become one of the leading applications. The presently changing and shifting paradigm in many fields of science, physics, database management and geometry considerably play a crucial role towards a massive change in the structure of finance sector, while being a major concern regarding cyber threat (Mosteanu & Faccia, 2021). The developing computing ability and the growth of elevating sturdy forecasting software provide competitive edge, important dynamics and computation of difficult problem. In this context, as previously mentioned, there is a greater probability of market concentration in which, although limited firms or the leader of innovations can afford to invest in these advancements, to gain competitive edge against their rival companies.

On the contrary side, it's crucial to monitor how quantum computers affect businesses and any potential negative effects or failures. For instance, companies must engage in investments to build their own quantum computing capabilities and evaluate the dangers and problems that could arise from this new technology.

Quantum Computers in Financial Markets

Quantum computing are determined to be at the developing phrase, currently as experiments have exhibited higher possibility of being beneficial in the finance sector. According to the estimated World Economic forum in 2022, government tend to finance around 25 billion USD in quantum-computing development and research as well as approximately 1 billion USD in deals of venture capitals were finalized in the current financial year (Szalavetz & Sauvage, 2023). The development of these computing innovations is at initial phrase, but on the other hand, there are various mechanical complexities which required to be resolved earlier before turning into actual instrument for routine utilization.

However, quantum computing has already exhibited higher possibility for utilization in extensive fields. Quantum computing has the capability to answer difficult arithmetical queries considerably in speed comparative to basic computers, turning this innovation as exemplary for various assignments. The finance division is topmost of the initial testers in developing the innovation although various other industries like logistics, military, manufacturing and pharmaceuticals are testing quantum computing.

The stated characteristics of quantum computing can have a prominent effect on the prospect of financial markets. There are various assignments and work where financial projection and financial modelling could be encouraged via quantum computing and greater precision procedures. Considerably, the optimization of portfolio, management of risk and pricing of assets are few of the highly quoted scenarios. Hence, their possible benefits and risks to cryptography turns it significant for financial markets to observe the innovation (Awan et al., 2022).

Alliance is vital in the field of quantum computing because of software and innovation evolution the transformation is possible. An increasing number of projects or schemes have been started via the biggest technology firms for trials with software, cloud solutions or hardware by the companies like Amazon, IBM, Microsoft or Google (Hashem et al., 2015).

Microsoft Azure Quantum has teamed with Goldman Sachs to discover the utilization of quantum computers for pricing. The quantum solutions are being experimented by JPMorgan for risk management and optimization. Likewise, HSBC has also collaborated with IBM to discover the quantum computer usefulness for pricing, reducing risk and optimization of portfolio (Fahlkvist & Kheiltash, 2023).

Quantum computers are categorized as a novel tool which operates on quantum mechanics fundamentals. This mechanic is an extension of physics which works in the field of matter behaviour and light on the atomic and subatomic scales (Tang et al., 2022). The highly prominent feature of quantum computer is that it can do calculations within a short period of time rather than basic computers.

Basic or fundamental computing machines process and store data in the bits unit whereas the quantum innovations utilize quantum bits (Qubits). The 'Bits' denotes data in a format of binary and can have just two probable values one or zero. Each piece of data which goes via a basic computer is necessarily an extended strand of ones and zeros.

The Qubits can survive in many states instantly, a feature referred as 'Superposition'. It denotes that an individual Qubit can exhibit various potential combinations of ones and zeros; thus, it can work with greater level of data comparative to just bits (Zanjirdar, 2020).

Another important characteristic of Qubits is their capacity for 'entanglement', in which two pairs of Qubits are coupled so that, irrespective of distance, the state of one directly impacts the state of the other. Transforming the level of one in the pair would deviate the level of the other Qubits in a forecastable manner. This feature provides supplementary competence to quantum computers. In a quantum computer, adding a Qubit results in processing power to increase exponentially, while increasing the number of bits in a classical computer results in a linear improvement in processing power.

On the other hand, performing tasks with Qubits is considerably a difficult task due to the fact that they require to be segregated in a restricted quantum state that is highly delicate. The tiniest deviation in the atmosphere physically can result in an unevenness, i.e. the superposition being collapsed. Tough safety actions are needed, like highly cooled refrigerators, vacuum chambers or insulations to shield the machine from imbalance of equilibrium.[7]

Second notion of the complexity is that as a dissimilar paradigm, quantum computers do not just need entirely unique software and hardware but solutions of algorithms. Various research studies have detailed the benefits of quantum computers in AI (artificial intelligence), cryptography and ML. No to very less consideration has been given to the point that it does not just refer the utilization of quantum computers to perform algorithms developed for basic computers while designing entirely novel algorithms, which are exploiting the quantum computer properties.

The probable effect of quantum computers on the banking sector is considerable because of their capability to manage the excessive level of transactions and estimations speedily (Albash & Lidar, 2018). Presently, few financial sectors are working with quantum algorithms, which control novel quantum features such as superposition and entanglement; however, the restrictions of these probabilities stay unattended.

A similar case is of Grover algorithms, which can be employed to find huge, unformed databases of financial information swiftly comparative to basic algorithms. Such as, it can be utilized to find for particular financial transactions or to recognize trends in financial information. Other case is Shor's algorithm which allows individual to factor in huge quantities greater speediness rather than basic algorithms.

For the optimization of portfolio, algorithms of Shor and Grover can be used (Gilliam et al., 2021). The Optimization of portfolio includes searching of the best possible combination of financing to gain maximum yield whereas reducing risk. Instead of offering speedier and greater precise computations, the innovation can offer more adaptable strategies for optimization which covers a broad range of elements, like governance indicators, social and environmental.

One more scenario could be pricing of asset. Pricing of asset is the procedure of computing the worth of financial assets like derivative, stocks or bonds. Customary techniques for financial assets pricing depends on complicated

---

[7]https://www.ibm.com/thought-leadership/institute-business-value/en-us/report/exploring-quantum-financial

arithmetic frameworks, like Simulations of Monte Carlo, which include imitating a massive number of probable results for a considered financial asset and then utilizing these imitations to measure its worth. QMC (quantum Monte Carlo) can manage, for instance, difficult financial tools, like options whose pay-offs are non-linear (Paudel et al., 2022).

The most common query regarding quantum computers is: can this computer forecast the stock market? Whereas quantum computers might have benefits above basic machines in some financial modelling assignments, it is less likely that it would be capable to forecast the stock market with greater precision. Furthermore, equally with any novel innovation, quantum computing additionally produces its own novel complexities and restriction which requires to be resolved earlier before its entire possibility in financial application could be noticed.

Various financial facilitation firms have higher hopes of quantum computers' impact on the management of risk. This includes searching, evaluating, classifying risk and taking measures to reduce or combat risky situations. Each phase includes arithmetic modelling and simulations for forecasting risk results and precision as well as duration contributes significantly in the procedure. The most crucial element of risk management is cybersecurity, which can be improved via developing more innovative methods of encryption.

In the financial sector, the encryption of data is the significant course of action which secures private and sensitive information from the access of unauthorized person or parties. This is applied to protect channels of communication among systems, apps, servers and websites. Second, encryption is need to produce signatures digitally which assist the assurance of document privacy and minimizes the risk of modification by unknown access.

Conclusively, quantum computers are not just loaded with benefits, but there are flaws as well for cryptography. Whereas it has the possibility to breach various of the present encryption techniques, it further has the capability to produce novel and more protected methods which are resistant to ambush via basic computers.

Quantum computers tend to be quick than basic computing machines, indicating that they can promptly answer arithmetic issues which fundamental computers would take decades, days or ages to figure out. It involves the arithmetic queries which support various of the encryption projects utilized to protect virtual transactions and communication.

For instance, the algorithms of Shor can be employed to effectively factor massive quantities, which is the ground for various public-key encryption algorithms like Rivest Shamir Adleman (RSA).

Hence, quantum cryptography could additionally be employed to design unique cryptographic techniques, which are reliable rather than basic techniques. As such, quantum key distribution is a technique to produce and allocate a private key among more than one party, the integrity and privacy of the data being trade could be secured though if an unauthorized party interrupts the communication.

The stated properties produce few instable situations in the prospect of quantum computing within blockchain innovations. It has the capability to pass through present encryption techniques employed in blockchain that can overlook the virtual assets and transactions privacy. Simultaneously, scholars and researchers are emphasizing on designing a quantum-proof encryption technique for blockchain to survive this attack, like Crystals Kyber public encryption key via IBM. Also, quantum computers can improve blockchain via elevating their performance time and reliability, which can increase their effectiveness and security of transactions.

Second, the financial markets and trading division might considerably witness a boost in effectiveness offered through the capability to develop greater sturdy algorithms which can conduct various estimations at the same time, expediting to a massive possibilities and forecasts being revealed regarding how markets are possibly to function (Zhang et al., 2022). Although the quantum computer has demonstrated its capability and ability in managing numerous financial issues, still difficulties occur because of the limited scale of present quantum-computing machines and the scarcity of a basic machine model for algorithms of quantum. The present analysis provides the overview for prospective observation.

Possible Assistances of Quantum Computing

The transformational power of quantum computers for financial markets due to their ability to answer various queries significantly speedy and precise rather than highly sturdy binary computers.

TheApplication of Quantum Computing in Finance

The key concepts of cryptography are derived from a variety of domains, including digital document signatures, fund transfers, and digital communication security. Utilizing quantum computers to eliminate cryptography might have a huge effect on economic operations. It is effortless to track this notion that an economy with absence of trustworthy electronic funds transfer and transactions of bank could impede. Hence, for prompt optimization and simulations, according to notion of utilitarian, elevated effectiveness in fields like allocation of resources, planning, medicine and materials development and ML could provide assistance.

The businesses adopting the quantum computer innovation for finance can enhance their status via decreasing fraudulent activities. For instance, Mastercard projected that its network has saved about 30 billion USD in fraud from past two years.[8] Additionally, for anti-money laundering there is also a technology for this purpose.

The schemes of fraudulent activity detection have to equalize the performance of real time against the number of properties which can be employed to estimate the possibility of financial transactions being authenticated. Quantum computers

---

[8]https://www.mastercard.com/news/press/2023/july/mastercard-leverages-its-ai-capabilities-to-fight-real-time-payment-scams/

provide more effective and efficient fraud detection by optimizing the selection of characteristics to ensure the usage of robust elements.

Optimization

In order to answer optimization issues on quantum related hardware, varied algorithms are recommended for distinct issues (Egger et al., 2020). For instance, the algorithms applied to resolve optimization issues in convex are dissimilar from the individuals answering discrete issues. In this case, quantum computers contribute significantly in optimization via providing quality solution and time for computation or both.

Potential benefits of quantum computers include improved computational speed and higher-quality solutions. The algorithms through which portfolios can be optimized or arbitrage alternatives could be found are some applications of multivariate issues where quantum-computers provide help due to their capability to assess various cases at once. Few of these issues are quadratic unconstrained binary optimization also known as QUBO issues which are usually executed through QAOA/VQE quantum-algorithms.

Monte Carlo Simulations

Such models are stochastic as they are implemented various times to compute the expected worth/value of risk analysis, options etc. The models' complexities and the goal certainty degree usually direct to colossal computations necessities on binary computers. QAE (Quantum-amplitude estimations) is a widely known quantum algorithms which assist match Monte Carlo techniques effectively and logically on a quantum computer (Ashtari et al., 2022).

Quantum Machine Learning

It can be utilized for principal component analysis, credit scoring and others.

The Management of Portfolio

The type of portfolio does not matter, but its complexity elevates with the amount of assets it acquires. Selecting a portfolio of which comprises of 10 assets from a list of potential 50 refers 10 billion dissimilar probable combinations. Accounting for supplementary elements, such as diverse trade arrangements, becomes intractable on a binary computer. Whereas quantum computers could not solve this task, it might be capable to recognize other optimal portfolios rather than present conventional optimizers; it would additionally be capable to do so quickly, offering greater rapid updates regarding portfolios.

Portfolio management through quantum computers can analyze the firm effect rapidly in use-cases like trading strategy optimization, index tracking for stock portfolio and managed collateral optimization. For example, quantum computers can assist forming strategies for trading to assess when to trade particular assets to attain a particular rate of return at a set level of risk. Customary optimization techniques generally evaluate millions of trading plans or schemes for multiple hours. When hardware gets mature enough, the optimization algorithms of quantum along quadratic speedups might be capable to considerably elevate the entire number of cases to evaluate and possibly identify improved strategies.

As per the analysis, if portfolio strategies powered by quantum computers could enhance an average return on financing around 1%–2% each year, these strategies will produce a supplementary 36 billion USD to 71 billion USD.[9] A likewise method can be utilized to optimize collateral management for the portfolio of loans. The entire risk and worth of these sort of portfolios are not just based on value and risk of each collateral assets, whereas additionally on their spread. Such as, if overall collateral in a loan portfolio is based on the similar guarantor or depends on securities in the similar sector, the entire risk of portfolio will be greater than if the collateral were greatly dissimilar. Effectively quantum-optimized loan portfolios which emphasize on collateral can offer financiers to enhance their proposing, probably reducing interest rate and freeing up funds.

Risk

Precisely handling varied types of risk is also a significant probable use. Reducing the overall risk of financial markets is among one the highly statistically exhausting tasks in financial markets and institutions as the risk is based on various elements. A precise projection of entire risk hence produces from processing a huge data reserve. Method of quantum computers can reduce the time duration for a nominal risk evaluation which applies a basic simulation of Monte Carlo for hours and days. Through processing greater samples promptly, this technique can in addition assist enhance the financial markets' accuracy to compute the risk. According to McKinsey, global leading financial markets collectively hold around 800 billion USD for a capital buffer, having a yearly expenditure of funds valued 80 billion USD. Greatly precise risk evaluation which minimizes this reserve via 1%–2% might release 0.8–1.6 billion USD each year. As per the analysts, this goal is practical, determining that saving of around 10% are already have been recognized with fundamental risk handling methods, free up the residual space for enhancement restricted via law.

Further, the management of risk is embedded for the complex derivative pricing and financial instruments whose prices are resulting from more than one underlying assets. The typical derivate contract pricing can occupy several hours; speedy pricing can hence could be a considerable competitive edge.

Quantum computer AI can be utilized to enhance the data feature selection, which decreases the variable number within a predictive framework to the highly

[9]https://www.mckinsey.com/industries/financial-services/our-insights/how-quantum-computing-could-change-financial-services

related ones. This expansion permits for the timely evaluation of big datasets, highly precise frameworks and swift reorientation for the ML framework. These instruments, specifically effectively training for ML frameworks, could be used for particular instruments in risk management. For example, higher precision credit scoring can decrease the risk of credit. An enhancement of 1%–2% in the worldwide default rate matches to a savings of 17–33 billion USD. This sum is similar to the possible revenue elevated via conventional risk analytics, i.e. 10 to 20 billion USD.

Whereas it is tough to compute the effect of quantum ML and AIto other fields of risk management, it is determined to influence the worth lost to card payment frauds, which is around 27.85 billion USD each year in 2018. Additional probable fields of influence are cyber-risk reduction and money-laundering detection, fields where industry professionals revealed that around 20 biggest financial markets presently incur expense 11 billion USD each year; a reduction of 1%–2% would help to secure 100 to 200 million USD. The influence of quantum ML is a disputed matter; whereas some professionals are doubtful because of a restricted quantity of practical use cases; others determine that in the prospect, quantum computers would have various high-value use cases. Due to its statistical intensity, professional consider that quantum risk management to be practical by end of 2030.

Summary

Quantum computers can assist to resolve and answer particular problems and issues that are not solvable by binary computers or classical hardware. Considering the prompt response offered by quantum computers, they have the possibility to assist any sector, market or division which utilizes estimations, such as financial markets. The use-cases like risk management, portfolio management and pricing of derivatives to provide insight about the usefulness of quantum computers in financial markets. This indicates that financial markets can benefit from quantum computers in the upcoming years.

The utilization of quantum computers provides various benefits in terms of portfolio optimization, risk management and other as the best possible combination of portfolios could be identified promptly. Whereas in case of Monte Carlo technique, it can be help for pricing derivatives and the projecting the level of risk like credit default risk. Specifically, prompt or high precision in pricing derivatives can considerably enhance the liquidity of financial markets, as well as the precise computation of risk management helps to reduce financial instability or uncertainty.

However, firms are experimenting with quantum computers, and there are different use-cases in the financial sector, but they vary in various levels. Thus, it is required to be considered that turning point in the growth of quantum computer hardware is vital to recognize the maximum capability of quantum-based algorithms for financial markets. For instance, excessive qubits are required and the errors of present hardware require to be minimized. The evolution of quantum computers is considerably tough which is another limitation due to which few studies are present on the effect on the finance sector. In order to witness these capabilities, quantum computers should be cost-effective and operated economically.

Learning Objectives

(1) What is quantum computing?
(2) The role of quantum computing in financial market.
(3) Applications of quantum computing employed in financial market.

References

A financial system that creates economic opportunities nonbank financials, fintech, and innovation. (2018, July). U.S. Department of the Treasury. https://home.treasury.gov/sites/default/files/2018-08/A-Financial-System-that-Creates-Economic-Opportunities%2D%2D-Nonbank-Financials-Fintech-and-Innovation.pdf

Agrawal, M., & Mishra, P. (2012). A comparative survey on symmetric key encryption techniques. *International Journal of Computer Science and Engineering*, *4*(5), 877.

Ahmadi, S. (2024). A comprehensive study on integration of big data and AI in financial industry and its effect on present and future opportunities. *International Journal of Current Science Research and Review*, *7*, 01.

Albareti, F. D., Ankenbrand, T., Bieri, D., Hänggi, E., Lötscher, D., Stettler, S., & Schöngens, M. (2022). A structured survey of quantum computing for the financial industry. arXiv preprint arXiv:2204.10026.

Albash, T., & Lidar, D. A. (2018). Adiabatic quantum computation. *Reviews of Modern Physics*, *90*(1), 015002.

Aldoseri, A., Al-Khalifa, K. N., & Hamouda, A. M. (2024). AI-powered innovation in digital transformation: Key pillars and industry impact. *Sustainability*, *16*(5), 1790.

Alexander, D. (2018, October 11). TD aims for 90% of transactions to be self-serve in digital push. *Bloomberg News*. https://www.bloomberg.com/news/articles/2018-10-11/td-aims-for-90-oftransactions-to-be-self-serve-in-digital-push

Allen, H. J. (2019). Regulatory sandboxes. *George Washington Law Review*, *87*, 579.

Anoshin, D., Matic, T., Bogdanovic, S., Lincoln, T., & Shirokov, D. (2019). *Tableau 2019. x Cookbook: Over 115 recipes to build end-to-end analytical solutions using Tableau*. Packt Publishing Ltd.

Arslanian, H. (2022). Bitcoin. In *The book of crypto: The complete guide to understanding bitcoin, cryptocurrencies and digital assets* (pp. 45–89). Springer International Publishing.

Arslanian, H., & Fischer, F. (2019). Applications of artificial intelligence in financial services. In *The future of finance* (pp. 179–197). Palgrave Macmillan.

Ashtari, S., Zhou, I., Abolhasan, M., Shariati, N., Lipman, J., & Ni, W. (2022). Knowledge-defined networking: Applications, challenges and future work. *Array*, *14*, 100136.

Athanassiou, P. (2011, August 9). Financial sector supervisors' accountability: A European perspective. ECB Legal Working Paper No. 12, SSRN. https://ssrn.com/abstract=1807174. http://dx.doi.org/10.2139/ssrn.1807174

Attico, N. (2020). *Blockchain ecosystem. Driving mass adoption*. goWare & Guerini Next. https://www.goware-apps.com/libri/blockchain-ecosystem-driving-mass-adoption-nicola-attico/

Auer, R. (2019, January 21). Beyond the doomsday economics of 'proof-of-work' in cryptocurrencies. BIS Working Paper No. 765, SSRN. https://ssrn.com/abstract=3331413

Aumasson, J. P. (2017). *Serious cryptography: A practical introduction to modern encryption*. No Starch Press.

Average overdraft fee | Increase in average overdraft fees, over time in the United States. (2016). Wiley. https://media.wiley.com/assets/7349/04/web-Accounts%20Average_Overdraft_Fee_US.png

Awan, U., Hannola, L., Tandon, A., Goyal, R. K., & Dhir, A. (2022). Quantum computing challenges in the software industry. A fuzzy AHP-based approach. *Information and Software Technology*, *147*, 106896.

Banking relationship in 2015 (U.S.). (2016) Wiley. https://media.wiley.com/assets/7350/52/web-Trust-Banking_Relationship_In_2015_US.png

Barros, A. R. (2008). How to make bankers richer: The Brazilian financial market with public and private banks. *The Quarterly Review of Economics and Finance*, *48*(2), 217–236.

Barth, J. R., Gan, J., & Nolle, D. E. (2009). Global banking regulation and supervision: What are the issues and what are the practices? Nova Science Publishers.

Belsky, E. S., & Essene, R. S. (2008). *Consumer and mortgage credit at a crossroads: Preserving expanded access while informing choices and protecting consumers.* Working Paper. Joint Center for Housing Studies, Harvard University.

Bell, C. J., Hogarth, J. M., & Robbins, E. (2009). *US households' access to and use of electronic banking, 1989–2007*. Federal Reserve Bulletin.

Bennett, C. H., & Brassard, G. (2020). Quantum cryptography: Public key distribution and coin tossing. arXiv preprint arXiv:2003.06557.

Bitcoin block reward halving countdown. https://www.bitcoinblockhalf.com/. Accessed on January 13, 2019.

Bitcoin History: The complete history of bitcoin [Timeline]. http://www.historyofbitcoin.org/. Accessed on February 13, 2023.

Bordo, M. D. (2003). Exchange rate regime choice in historical perspective. IMF Working Papers, Vol No. 03/160.

Borghard, E. (2018, September 24). Protecting financial institutions against cyber threats: A national security issue. Carnegie Endowment for International Peace (blog). https://carnegieendowment. org/2018/09/24/protecting-financial-institutions-against-cyber-threats-national-security-issuepub-77324

Bouland, A., van Dam, W., Joorati, H., Kerenidis, I., & Prakash, A. (2020). Prospects and challenges of quantum finance. arXiv preprint arXiv:2011.06492.

Brewster, K. (2023). The importance of data Analytics for financial services. https://www.brewsterconsulting.io/the-importance-of-data-analytics-for-financial-services

Bromby, M. (2010). Identification, trust and privacy: How biometrics can aid certification of digital signatures. *International Review of Law, Computers & Technology*, *24*(1), 133–141.

Bughin, J., Catlin, T., Hirt, M., & Willmott, P. (2018, January). Why digital strategies fail. McKinsey. https://www.mckinsey.com/business-functions/digital-mckinsey/our-insights/why-digital-strategies-fail

Burniske, C., & Tatar, J. (2018). Cryptoassets: The innovative investor's guide to Bitcoin and beyond. McGraw-Hill.

Chandra, S., Bhattacharyya, S., Paira, S., & Alam, S. S. (2014, November). A study and analysis on symmetric cryptography. In *2014 International Conference on Science Engineering and Management Research (ICSEMR)* (pp. 1–8). IEEE.

Chauhan, V., Negi, S., Jain, D., Singh, P., Sagar, A. K., & Sharma, A. K. (2022, April). Quantum computers: A review on how quantum computing can boom AI. In *2022 2nd International Conference on Advance Computing and Innovative Technologies in Engineering (ICACITE)* (pp. 559–563). IEEE.

Cheng, E. (2017, November 26). Bitcoin tops $8,700 to record high as coinbase adds 100,000 users. *CNBC*. https://www.cnbc.com/2017/11/25/bitcoin-tops-8700-to-record-high-as-coinbase-adds-100000-users.html

Chiu, I. H. (2011). Institutional shareholders as stewards: Toward a new conception of corporate governance. *Brooklyn Journal of Corporate, Financial & Commercial Law*, *6*, 387.

Citi. (2018, March). *Bank of the future – The ABCs of digital disruption in finance*. Citi Global Perspectives & Solutions (Citi GPS). https://www.citibank.com/commercialbank/insights/assets/ docs/2018/The-Bank-of-the-Future/124/

Collinson, P. (2013, September 7). Switching banks: Why are we more loyal to our bank than to a partner? *The Guardian*. https://www.theguardian.com/money/2013/sep/07/switchingbanks-seven-day

Confirmed transactions per day. Blockchain.com. https://www.blockchain.com/charts/n-transactions. Accessed on January 13, 2019.

Corporate Finance Institute. (2023). Big data in finance- definition, uses, challenges. https://corporatefinanceinstitute.com/resources/data-science/big-data-in-finance/#:~:text=Summary-,Big%20data%20in%20finance%20refers%20to%20large%2C%20diverse%20(structured%20and,to%20long%2Dstanding%20business%20challenges

Crittenden, A. B., Crittenden, V. L., & Crittenden, W. F. (2019). The digitalization triumvirate: How incumbents survive. *Business Horizons*, *62*(2), 259–266.

Dam, K. W. (2009). The subprime crisis and financial regulation: International and comparative perspectives. *Chicago Journal of International Law*, *10*, 581.

Das, U., & Quintyn, M. (2002, September). Crisis prevention and crisis management the role of regulatory governance. IMF Working Paper No. 02/163, SSRN. https://ssrn.com/abstract=880183

Davies, H., & Green, D. (2013). *Global financial regulation: The essential guide* (Now with a Revised Introduction). John Wiley & Sons.

de la Torre, I., Torralba, L., & Rivera, J. (2018). The Fintech revolution. https://www.ignaciodelatorre.com/wp-content/uploads/2020/04/20181030_The-Fintech-Revolution.pdf

Dechand, S., Naiakshina, A., Danilova, A., & Smith, M. (2019, June). In encryption we don't trust: The effect of end-to-end encryption to the masses on user perception. In *2019 IEEE European Symposium on Security and Privacy (EuroS&P)* (pp. 401–415). IEEE.

Del Mar, A. (1902). *A history of the precious metals: From the earliest times to the present*. Cambridge Encyclopedia Company.

Derman, E., & Miller, M. B. (2016). *The volatility smile*. John Wiley & Sons.

Desai, P. (2011). *From financial crisis to global recovery*. Columbia University Press.

Dodd, R. (2012). What are money markets? *Finance & Development*, *46*.

Duckenfield, M. (2016). The rise of the gold standard, 1660–1819. In *The monetary history of gold* (pp. 1–154). Routledge.

Duignan, B. (Ed.). (2012). *Money and capital*. Britannica Educational Publishing.

Edward Snowden. (2023, February 23). Wikipedia. https://en.wikipedia.org/wiki/Edward_Snowden

Egger, D. J., Gambella, C., Marecek, J., McFaddin, S., Mevissen, M., Raymond, R., Simonetto, A., Woerner, S., & Yndurain, E. (2020). Quantum computing for finance: State-of-the-art and future prospects. *IEEE Transactions on Quantum Engineering*, *1*, 1–24.

Ellul, A. (2015). The role of risk management in corporate governance. *Annual Review of Financial Economics*, *7*(1), 279–299.

Elwell, C. K. (2011). Brief history of the gold standard (GS) in the United States. Congressional Research Service.

Eriksen, L. L. R., & Alne, M. C. (2019). *In the wake of the revised payment services directive: A study on how Norwegian banks are responding to PSD2, and how their competitive relationships and roles are affected in consequence* (Master's thesis).

Fahlkvist, A., & Kheiltash, A. (2023). The impact of quantum computing on the financial sector: Exploring the current performance and prospects of quantum computing for financial applications through mean-variance optimization (dissertation). https://urn.kb.se/resolve?urn=urn:nbn:se:liu:diva-196213

Farell, R. (2015). An analysis of the cryptocurrency industry. *Wharton Research Scholars*, *130*, 1–23.

Feuerriegel, S., Hartmann, J., Janiesch, C., & Zschech, P. (2024). Generative ai. *Business & Information Systems Engineering*, *66*(1), 111–126.

Fox, S. (2013). *51% of US adults bank online* (p. 2). Pew Research Center.

Garicano, L., & Lastra, R. M. (2010). Towards a new architecture for financial stability: Seven principles. *Journal of International Economic Law*, *13*(3), 597–621.

Gilliam, A., Woerner, S., & Gonciulea, C. (2021). Grover adaptive search for constrained polynomial binary optimization. *Quantum*, *5*, 428.

Girasa, R. (2018). Regulation of cryptocurrencies and blockchain technologies. In *National and international perspectives. Suiza*. Palgrave Macmillan.

Gorton, G. (2015). *The maze of banking: History, theory, crisis*. Oxford University Press.

Grosse, R. (1997). The future of the global financial services industry. *International Executive*, *39*(5), 599–617.

Gupta, S., & Sharma, V. (2023, May). Effects of quantum computing on businesses. In *2023 4th International Conference on Intelligent Engineering and Management (ICIEM)* (pp. 1–6). IEEE.

Hadmi, A., Puech, W., Said, B. A. E., & Ouahman, A. A. (2013). A robust and secure perceptual hashing system based on a quantization step analysis. *Signal Processing: Image Communication*, *28*(8), 929–948.

Hashem, I. A. T., Yaqoob, I., Anuar, N. B., Mokhtar, S., Gani, A., & Khan, S. U. (2015). The rise of "big data" on cloud computing: Review and open research issues. *Information Systems*, *47*, 98–115.

Hassija, V., Chamola, V., Saxena, V., Chanana, V., Parashari, P., Mumtaz, S., & Guizani, M. (2020). Present landscape of quantum computing. *IET Quantum Communication*, *1*(2), 42–48.

Herman, D., Googin, C., Liu, X., Galda, A., Safro, I., Sun, Y., Pistoia, M., & Alexeev, Y. (2022). A survey of quantum computing for finance. arXiv preprint arXiv:2201.02773.

Hileman, G. (2016, January 28). *State of bitcoin and blockchain 2016: Blockchain hits critical mass.* CoinDesk. https://www.coindesk.com/state-of-bitcoin-blockchain-2016

Hines, B. (2020). *Digital finance: Security tokens and unlocking the real potential of blockchain.* John Wiley & Sons.

Howcroft, B., Hamilton, R., & Paul, H. (2002). Consumer attitude and the usage and adoption of home-based banking in the United Kingdom. *International Journal of Bank Marketing*, *20*(3), 111–121.

IANS. (2018, September 21). *Globally, just half of retail bank customers happy with services: Report.* Business Standard India. https://www.business-standard.com/article/finance/globally-just-half-ofretail-bank-customers-happy-with-services-report-118092100610_1.html

Igan, D., & Lambert, T. (2018). Bank lobbying: Regulatory capture and beyond. Available at SSRN 3128829.

IIMJ. (2023). Data analytics in banking and financial services. https://www.iimj.ac.in/omdp3-2023

InterSystem. (2022). A glimpse at the top data challenges in financial servies technology. https://www.linkedin.com/pulse/glimpse-top-data-challenges-financial-services-technology-/

Ismail, A. M. (2013). *Development of a corporate integrity assessment instrument using corporate governance indicators in Malaysia.* Doctoral dissertation. Victoria University.

Judmayer, A., Stifter, N., Krombholz, K., & Weippl, E. (2022). *Blocks and chains: Introduction to bitcoin, cryptocurrencies, and their consensus mechanisms.* Springer Nature.

Küfeoglu, S., & Özkuran, M. (2019). Energy consumption of bitcoin mining. https://doi.org/10.17863/CAM.41230

Kambies, T., Mittal, N., & Sharma, S. K. (2017, February 7). *Analyzing dark data for hidden opportunities.* Deloitte Insights. https://www2.deloitte.com/insights/us/en/focus/tech-trends/2017/dark-data-analyzing- unstructured-data. html

Kaptan, S. S. (2002). *New concepts in banking.* Sarup & Sons.

Laszlo Hanyecz. Bitcoin Wiki. https://en.bitcoin.it/wiki/Laszlo_Hanyecz. Accessed on January 13, 2019.

Lechman, E. (2013). New technologies adoption and diffusion patterns in developing countries. An empirical study for the period 2000–2011. *Equilibrium. Quarterly Journal of Economics and Economic Policy*, *8*(4), 79–106.

Lee, B. (2018). Deriving the derivative. *Signs and Society*, *6*(1), 225–255.

Light, P. C. (2011). *Monitoring government: Inspectors general and the search for accountability.* Brookings Institution Press.

Liu, Z., Yang, G., Wong, D. S., Nguyen, K., & Wang, H. (2019, June). Key-insulated and privacy-preserving signature scheme with publicly derived public key. In *2019 IEEE European Symposium on Security and Privacy (EuroS&P)* (pp. 215–230). IEEE.

Loizou, P., & French, N. (2012). Risk and uncertainty in development: A critical evaluation of using the Monte Carlo simulation method as a decision tool in real estate development projects. *Journal of Property Investment & Finance*, *30*(2), 198–210.

Macey, J. R. (2003). Regulatory globalization as a response to regulatory competition. *Emory LJ*, *52*, 1353.

Magnuson, W. (2018). Regulating fintech. *Vanderbilt Law Review*, *71*, 1167.

Marous, J. (2017, February 6). Banking needs a customer experience wake-up call. The Financial Brand. https://thefinancialbrand.com/63654/banking-customer-experience-research-survey/

McCandless, G. T. (1996). Money, expectations, and the US Civil War. *The American Economic Review*, *86*(3), 661–671.

McCardel, K. (2022). The impact of Edward Snowden on data protections, individual privacy, and ontological security. Univerzita Karlova, Fakulta sociálních věd.

McDermott, P. (2010). Building open government. *Government Information Quarterly*, *27*(4), 401–413.

McKinsey and Company. (2023). The state of AI in 2023: Generative AI's breakout year. https://www.mckinsey.com/capabilities/quantumblack/our-insights/the-state-of-ai-in-2023-generative-ais-breakout-year

Mehrpouya, A., & Djelic, M. L. (2014). *Transparency: From enlightenment to neoliberalism or when a norm of liberation becomes a tool of governing*. HEC Paris Research Paper No. ACC-2014-1059.

Möller, M., & Vuik, C. (2017). On the impact of quantum computing technology on future developments in high-performance scientific computing. *Ethics and Information Technology*, *19*, 253–269.

Moloney, N. (2023). *EU securities and financial markets regulation*. Oxford University Press.

MONIKA POHLE, R. A. S. E. R. (2007). From the Athenian Tetradrachm to the Euro. Routledge.

Moreno, S. M., Seigneur, J. M., & Gotzev, G. (2021). A survey of KYC/AML for cryptocurrencies transactions. In *Handbook of research on cyber crime and information privacy* (pp. 21–42). IGI Global.

Mosteanu, N. R., & Faccia, A. (2021). Fintech frontiers in quantum computing, fractals, and blockchain distributed ledger: Paradigm shifts and open innovation. *Journal of Open Innovation: Technology, Market, and Complexity*, *7*(1), 19.

Mundell, R. A. (2002). The birth of coinage. *Zagreb Journal of Economics*, *3*(4), 5–55.

Nabilou, H. (2019). How to regulate bitcoin? Decentralized regulation for a decentralized cryptocurrency. *International Journal of Law and Info Technology*, *27*(3), 266–291.

Nagaoka, H., Ukai, Y., & Takemura, T. (2005). Past and present of information systems in banks. *Economic Analysis of Information System Investment in Banking Industry*, 3–28.

Nakamoto, 2009 Nakamoto, S. (2009). Bitcoin: A peer-to-peer electronic cash system bitcoin: A peer-to-peer electronic cash system. Bitcoin. org. https://bitcoin. org/en/bitcoin-paper

Nakamoto, S., & Bitcoin, A. (2008). A peer-to-peer electronic cash system. *Bitcoin*, *4*(2), 15. https://bitcoin. org/bitcoin. pdf

Nanto, D. K. (2009). *The global financial crisis: Analysis and policy implications*. Diane Publishing.

Nielsen, M. A., & Chuang, I. L. (2010). *Quantum computation and quantum information*. Cambridge University Press.

O'Bryan, J. (2013). A history of weapons: Crossbows, caltrops, catapults & lots of other things that can seriously mess you up. Chronicle Books.

Ordemann, D. (2017). Why robotics-led finance could signal the dawn of a new partnership. https://www.ey.com/en_bg/assurance/why-robotics-led-finance-could-signal-the-dawn-of-a-new-partners

Orús, R., Mugel, S., & Lizaso, E. (2019). Quantum computing for finance: Overview and prospects. *Reviews in Physics*, *4*, 100028.

Osma, B. G., Mora, A., & Porcuna-Enguix, L. (2019). Prudential supervisors' independence and income smoothing in European banks. *Journal of Banking & Finance*, *102*, 156–176.

Pachghare, V. K. (2019). *Cryptography and information security*. PHI Learning Pvt. Ltd.

Packin, N. G. (2020). Show me the (data about the) money! *Utah Law Review*, *1277*.

Papanagnou, C. I. (2007). *Modelling, optimisation and control of series supply chains and production processes*. Doctoral dissertation. City University London.

Paudel, H. P., Syamlal, M., Crawford, S. E., Lee, Y. L., Shugayev, R. A., Lu, P., Ohodnicki, P. R., Mollot, D., & Duan, Y. (2022). Quantum computing and simulations for energy applications: Review and perspective. *ACS Engineering Au*, *2*(3), 151–196.

Peden, G. C. (1983). The treasury as the central department of government, 1919–1939. *Public Administration*, *61*(4), 371–385.

Peng, S. (2013). *Bitcoin: Cryptography, economics, and the future*. Senior Capstone Thesis. School of Engineering and Applied Science.

Policy Responses to the Global Financial Crisis (Financial Economics). (n.d.). tutor2u. https://www.tutor2u.net/economics/reference/financial-economics-policy-responses-to-the-global-financial-crisis

Pollitt, C., & Talbot, C. (Eds.). (2003). *Unbundled government*. Routledge.

Prager, J. (2013). The financial crisis of 2007/8: Misaligned incentives, bank mismanagement, and troubling policy implications. *Economics, Management, and Financial Markets*, *8*(2), 11–56.

Prodromou, T. (2020). Online banking: Factors that affect or influence internet banking, consumer perceived risk and attitude. https://kypseli.ouc.ac.cy/handle/11128/4670

Qi, Y., & Xiao, J. (2018). Fintech: AI powers financial services to improve people's lives. *Communications of the ACM*, *61*(11), 65–69.

Quintyn, M. (2007). *Governance of financial supervisors and its effects–A stocktaking exercise* (No. 2007/4). SUERF studies.

Quintyn, M., & Taylor, M. (2007, Janurary). Building supervisory structures in Sub-Saharan Africa-an analytical framework. IMF Working Paper No. 07/18, SSRN. https://ssrn.com/abstract=961092

Rani, S., & Kaur, H. (2017). Technical review on symmetric and asymmetric cryptography algorithms. *International Journal of Advanced Research in Computer Science*, *8*(4).

Rofe, J. S. (2017). *Global perspectives on the Bretton Woods conference and the post-war world order*. Palgrave Macmillan.

Royal, J. Bitcon price history: 2009 to 2024. https://www.bankrate.com/investing/bitcoin-price-history/

Scott, B. A., Amel, E. L., Koger, S. M., & Manning, C. M. (2021). *Psychology for sustainability*. Routledge.

Schar, F., & Berentsen, A. (2020). *Bitcoin, blockchain, and cryptoassets: A comprehensive introduction*. MIT Press.

Scott, H. S. (1998). When the euro falls apart. *International Finance*, *1*(2), 207–228.

Selimoglu, S. K., & Saldi, M. H. (2023). Blockchain technology for internal audit in cyber security governance of banking sector in Turkey: A SWOT analysis. In *Contemporary studies of risks in emerging technology, Part B* (pp. 23–55). Emerald Publishing Limited.

Shelanski, H., Knox, S., & Dhilla, A. (2017, June 21). *Network effects and efficiencies in multisided markets*. Organisation for Economic Co-operation and Development. https://one.oecd.org/document/DAF/COMP/WD(2017)40/FINAL/en/pdf

Shi, N. (2016). A new proof-of-work mechanism for bitcoin. *Financial Innovation*, *2*, 1–8.

Soni, J. (2022). *The founders: The story of paypal and the entrepreneurs who shaped silicon valley*. Simon & Schuster.

Stein, J. C. (2012). Monetary policy as financial stability regulation. *Quarterly Journal of Economics*, *127*(1), 57–95.

Su, E. (2020). Money market mutual funds: A financial stability case study

Sundar, R., & Suguna, A. (2024). *Introduction to digital entrepreneurs and digital business management*. Academic Guru Publishing House.

Szalavetz, A., & Sauvage, N. (2023). The financialization of corporate venture capital investment? The corporation as a venture capitalist. *Socio-Economic Review*, mwad036.

Tang, Y., Yan, J., Hu, G., Zhang, B., & Zhou, J. (2022). Recent progress and perspectives on quantum computing for finance. *Service Oriented Computing and Applications*, *16*(4), 227–229.

Thompson, P. (2018, June 2). Bitcoin mining's electricity bill: Is it worth it? *Cointelegraph*. https://cointelegraph.com/news/bitcoin-minings-electricity-bill-is-it-worth-it

Toteva, G. D. (2005). *Local cultures of late Achaemenid Anatolia*. Doctoral dissertation. University of Minnesota.

Trefis Team. (2017, August 24). Five largest ETF providers manage almost 90% of the $3 trillion U.S. ETF industry. *Forbes*. https://www.forbes.com/sites/greatspeculations/2017/08/24/five-largest-etfproviders-manage-almost-90-of-the-3-trillion-u-s-etf-industry/

Triffin, R. (1978). *Gold and the dollar crisis: Yesterday and tomorrow*. No. 132. International Finance Section, Department of Economics, Princeton University.

UBS, A. (2008, April 18). Shareholder report on UBS's write-downs. *UBS AG, Zurich*. https://maths-fi.com/ubs-shareholder-report.pdf

Vaclav, P. (2023). How can you use Data Mining to identify and mitigate financial risks? https://www.linkedin.com/advice/1/how-can-you-use-data-mining-identify-mitigate-financial-jfs6c#:~:text=Data%20mining%20can%20help%20you%20assess%20the%20creditworthiness%20of%20potential,%2C%20credit%20history%2C%20and%20collateral

Van Asselt, M. B., & Renn, O. (2011). Risk governance. *Journal of Risk Research, 14*(4), 431–449.

Varma, P., Nijjer, S., Sood, K., Grima, S., & Rupeika-Apoga, R. (2022). Thematic analysis of financial technology (Fintech) influence on the banking industry. *Risks, 10*, 186.

Vidal, M., & Vidal-García, J. (2016). Online banking. In *International perspectives on socio-economic development in the era of globalization* (pp. 185–201). IGI Global.

Vinothiyalakshmi, P., Muralidharan, C., Sirajudeen, Y. M., & Anitha, R. (2022). Digitized land registration using blockchain technology. In *Blockchain technology* (pp. 73–86). CRC Press.

Viola, L. A. (2013). The G-20 and global financial regulation. In *Handbook of global economic governance* (pp. 115–128). Routledge.

Waupsh, J. (2016). *Bankruption: How community banking can survive Fintech.* John Wiley & Sons.

Wewege, L., Lee, J., & Thomsett, M. C. (2020). Disruptions and digital banking trends. *Journal of Applied Finance and Banking, 10*(6), 15–56.

Wheelock, D. C., & Wilson, P. (2004, September/October). *Trends in the efficiency of federal reserve check processing operations* (p. 86). Federal Reserve Bank of St. Louis Review.

Wiley: Bankruption companion site content. (2016, November). Wiley. https://www.wiley.com/WileyCDA/Section/id-829480.html

Yackee, J. W., & Yackee, S. W. (2016). From legislation to regulation: An empirical examination of agency responsiveness to congressional delegations of regulatory authority. *Administrative Law Review, 68*, 395.

Zanjirdar, M. (2020). Overview of portfolio optimization models. *Advances in mathematical finance and applications, 5*(4), 419–435.

Zhang, X., Pan, G., Chen, B. B., Li, H., Sun, K., & Meng, Z. Y. (2022). Quantum Monte Carlo sign bounds, topological Mott insulator and thermodynamic transitions in twisted bilayer graphene model. arXiv preprint arXiv:2210.11733.

2018 U.S. Retail banking satisfaction study. (2018, April 26). J.D. Power. https://www.jdpower.com/business/press-releases/jd-power-2018-us-retail-banking-satisfaction-study

Index

Printed and bound by CPI Group (UK) Ltd, Croydon, CR0 4YY

15/09/2026

14962489-0008